CW01044418

PRESTON to the FYLDE COAST

Steam - Diesel - Electric
featuring Blackpool and Fleetwood

Tom Heavyside

MP Middleton Press

Front cover: A bygone era. With the unmistakable Blackpool Tower rising above the North station's concourse on the right, class 47 no. 47016 awaits departure time with the 17.58 service to Manchester Victoria on 18th June 1988. The loco and coaches were substituting for an unavailable diesel multiple-unit. The scene was completely transformed in 2018 with the rebuilding of the station platforms, and the advent of electric trains. (Tom Heavyside)

Back cover picture: Since the banishment of steam traction on normal services on British Railways in 1968, steam preservation on the Fylde has had mixed fortunes. Here Edward Borrows 0-4-0 well tank The King, *built in 1906, hauls a couple of goods vehicles along some rather overgrown track, on what proved the last day of operating at the short-lived Fleetwood Locomotive Centre on 2nd September 1997. Today the loco can be seen at the Ribble Steam Railway in Preston. (Tom Heavyside)*

Back cover map: Railway Clearing House map (edited), dated 1947. The route of the album is shown with a dotted line.

PRELUDE

This is a second book in the 'Evolving the Ultimate Rail Encyclopedia' series featuring the railways west of Preston, *Preston to Blackpool including Fleetwood* being first published in 2018. The latter mainly concentrated on the changing scene up until 1990, since which time the railways across the Fylde have undergone some radical changes, both as regards infrastructure as well as the motive power. This volume details the last years of steam workings in the 1960s, the period when diesel power monopolised the services, along with the current scene following electrification of the line to Blackpool North in 2018. Included also are a few private industrial railway sites, along with a look at some early railway preservation schemes.

Published November 2023

ISBN 978 1 910356 81 4

© Middleton Press Ltd, 2023

Cover design and Photographic enhancement
  Deborah Esher
Production Cassandra Morgan

Published by
  Middleton Press Ltd
  Camelsdale Road
  Haslemere
  Surrey
  GU27 3RJ
Tel: 01730 813169
Email: info@middletonpress.co.uk
www.middletonpress.co.uk

Printed and bound by CPI Group (UK) Ltd, Croydon, CR0 4YY

Railway company abbreviations:
Blackpool & Lytham Railway (B&LR)
British Railways (BR)
Lancashire & Yorkshire Railway (L&YR)
London Midland & Scottish Railway (LMS)
London & North Western (LNWR)
North Union Railway (NUR)
Preston & Wyre Railway (P&WR)

SECTIONS

1. Preset to Blackpool Central   1-74
2. Kirkham & Wesham to Fleetwood   75-103
3. Poulton-le-Fylde to Blackpool North   104-120

CONTENTS

50	Ansdell & Fairhaven	44	Lytham Goods
70	Blackpool Central	41	Lytham Motive Power Museum
68	Blackpool Engine Shed	38	Moss Side
112	Blackpool North	57	Pleasure Island
110	Blackpool North Engine Shed	80	Poulton Goods
61	Blackpool Pleasure Beach	81	Poulton-le-Fylde
64	Blackpool South	1	Preston
92	Burn Naze	9	Preston Engine Shed
102	Fleetwood	18	Royal Ordnance Springfields Factory
96	Fleetwood Engine Shed	53	St Annes-on-the-Sea
94	Fleetwood Locomotive Centre	21	Salwick
90	ICI Hillhouse Works	58	Squires Gate
24	Kirkham & Wesham	87	Thornton-Cleveleys
108	Layton	36	Wrea Green
46	Lytham	99	Wyre Dock

I. The Railway Clearing House map (edited) of 1947 has the route of this album in dark grey.

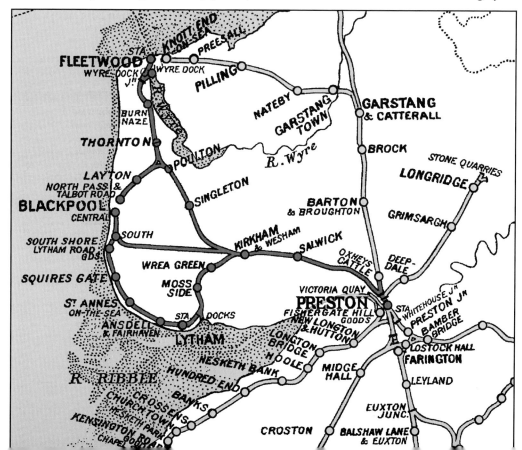

ACKNOWLEDGEMENTS

I am indebted to all who have enhanced this volume by their photographs which are acknowledged individually. In addition I should mention the ready help received from Peter Barber, Paul Chancellor, Godfrey Croughton, Geoff Gartside, Chris Howard, Eddie Johnson, Norman Langridge, Michael Lomax, Peter Mooney, Mike Norris, David Postle, David Salter, Dr Susan Salter, Paul Shackcloth, Paul Shannon, Keith Smith and Michael Stewart. Sincere thanks, too, to the team at Middleton Press, Deborah, Ray and Cass, who maintain and continue to expand the series founded by the late Vic Mitchell, and with whom the idea for this volume was first conceived.

GEOGRAPHICAL SETTING

Our excursion starts at the ancient borough of Preston at the heart of Lancashire, its charter having been granted by Henry II in 1179. Known in more recent times for its once thriving cotton industry, it is now a major bustling city, as well as the administrative centre for the county. It is strategically located at the mouth of the River Ribble, its waters flowing down from its source high in the Pennines, near the famed Ribblehead viaduct on the Settle & Carlisle line, into the Irish Sea.

From Preston we journey west across the flat-lands of the Fylde peninsula towards our main destination, the incomparable often booming seaside resort of Blackpool, its myriad entertainment establishments catering for fun-seekers of widely differing tastes. Those of a genteel disposition often favour the far more sedate surrounds of Lytham and St Annes, on the north bank of the Ribble estuary. Further north along the coast Fleetwood, at the mouth of the River Wyre, could once claim to be one of the most important fishing ports on the west coast of Britain. These days the towns hugging the Fylde coastline are quite densely populated, with numbers swelled considerably during most of the year by a vibrant tourist industry.

Inland the area is largely rural and given over to agriculture, mainly dairy with some arable and poultry farming. Beneath the surface are vast deposits of red sandstone, which in recent times has been seen as a source of gas. Despite much local opposition a start was made on sinking test boreholes for fracking in late 2018, but the exercise was soon abandoned, the Government placing a moratorium on such drilling the following year.

The maps are all to the scale of 6ins to 1 mile as surveyed in 1954-56 (some slightly reduced), except for Preston, Salwick and Kirkham, which are from the 1960-68 editions.

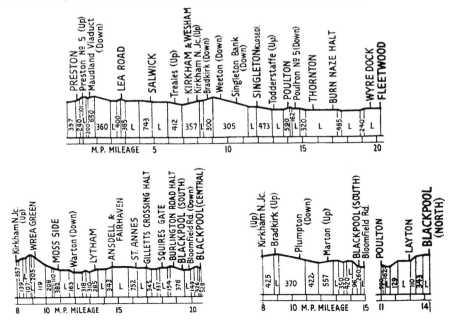

HISTORICAL BACKGROUND

The first railway across the Fylde was the Preston & Wyre Railway (P&WR), opened from Maudlands (half-a-mile north of the present Preston station) to the recently established town of Fleetwood on 15th July 1840. With the North Union Railway (NUR) having reached Preston from the south two years earlier on 31st October 1838, the P&WR provided the most convenient way of reaching Scotland, by means of connecting steamers from Fleetwood to Ardrossan on the Ayrshire coast. However the opening of the West Coast main line over Shap to Carlisle in 1846 and onward to Glasgow in 1848, meant the P&WR route to Scotland was relatively short-lived.

Meanwhile the P&WR had expanded its territory when it opened a line from a junction one mile west of Kirkham to Lytham on 16th February 1846, and two months later on 29th April, to Blackpool by means of a branch which left the Fleetwood line at Poulton. Subsequently the P&WR became jointly vested in the Lancashire & Yorkshire (L&YR, two-thirds) and London & North Western (LNWR, one-third) railways on 28th July 1849.

Next on the scene was the Blackpool & Lytham Railway (B&LR), which began business on 6th April 1863. This too became the joint property of the L&YR and LNWR on 1st July 1871. Three years later on 1st July 1874 a more direct line was opened between Kirkham and Wrea Green, and on the same day the former P&WR line at Lytham was extended to the ex-B&LR terminus to provide a second through route to Blackpool.

Further major engineering work was undertaken during 1888-89 when the line between Preston and Kirkham was quadrupled, followed by a major remodelling of the layout at Poulton, finished in March 1896. Additional projects saw a link laid between the Blackpool and Fleetwood lines at Poulton open on 1st July 1899, while the direct line between Kirkham and Waterloo Road (Blackpool) was first used in April 1903. This was usually referred to as the Marton line; Marton being a suburb of Blackpool. This completed the basic infrastructure that was later handed down to the London Midland & Scottish Railway (LMS) at the Grouping of the railways in January 1923 (the L&YR having been absorbed by the LNWR in January 1922), and subsequently to British Railways upon Nationalisation in January 1948.

Under BR little changed until autumn 1964, following the controversial report as to the future of the railways by Dr Beeching the previous year. This recommended closure of the line between Poulton and Blackpool North, but after strong representations from Blackpool Corporation, it was agreed to retain the route to North station, with Central closing instead on 2nd November 1964. From this date Blackpool South became a terminal station, with the vacated land between South and Central stations purchased by the council for redevelopment. The direct passenger service between Blackpool North and Fleetwood was also ended on 2nd November 1964.

With declining traffic the above heralded a number of rationalisation schemes, with first the fast lines between Preston and Kirkham being taken out of use on 15th November 1965. Next the Fleetwood branch was shortened when the line beyond Wyre Dock was abandoned on 18th April 1966. The Marton line officially closed in February 1967, although it had not been used as a through route since the previous summer. Then from May 1970 Blackpool North became recognised as the main station in the town when the Manchester and London trains were diverted from Blackpool South, leaving just a basic service along the coast line. The passenger service between Poulton and Wyre Dock was withdrawn on 1st June 1970, with goods traffic continuing as far as Burn Naze until 1999.

Following privatisation local services across the Fylde were operated by North Western Trains from March 1997 (First North Western from November 1998), Northern Rail and TransPennine Express from December 2004 (the latter providing trains to Manchester Airport). Arriva Northern took over in May 2016. In addition Virgin Trains ran limited services to London Euston and Portsmouth Harbour from May 1998 until May 2003 and Euston again from December 2014.

West of Preston all lines were closed from 11th November 2017 to facilitate electrification of the route to Blackpool North, with overhead wires energised at 25kV as on the West Coast main line. Preston to Blackpool South reopened on 29th January 2018 and Kirkham to Blackpool North on 20th May. At the same time all remaining manual signal boxes were abolished with control transferred to the Manchester Rail Operating Centre.

Avanti West Coast became responsible for London services on 8th December 2019, while from 1st March 2020 other services to Blackpool have been provided by the publicly-owned Northern Trains as the Government's Operator of Last Resort.

PASSENGER SERVICES

The Fylde Coast has always been well-served by rail. The table below details the number of departures each day for selected years during the period under review from Blackpool North and South stations. The figures highlight the growing importance of North compared to South, as well as the much improved Sunday services.

	Blackpool North			Blackpool South		
	Weekdays	**Saturdays**	**Sundays**	**Weekdays**	**Saturdays**	**Sundays**
1965	21	43	15	24	28	12
1982	35	51	23	14	13	none
2000	63	64	52	17	17	12
2023	75	74	46	19	19	13

From Fleetwood in 1965 there were 18 departures on Mondays to Saturdays, but none on Sundays.

To be factored in during the 1960s was a veritable host of excursion traffic and reliefs from seemingly all points north, south and east, that taxed the infrastructure to capacity most weekends and bank holidays. These began to converge on Blackpool from Eastertide through to the end of October/beginning of November, when the famed 'Illuminations' along the Promenade were switched off. The number of specials and timetabled weekend services declined rapidly from the mid-1960s: some of the starting/destination stations of these trains are mentioned in the captions. Today specials are a rarity.

Over the years Manchester, Liverpool and east Lancashire have been the main regular destinations for trains from Blackpool, with usually a limited service provided to London Euston. In 2023 there were twice hourly departures from North station to Manchester Airport, and hourly to Liverpool Lime Street and York, with three to Euston. Departures from Blackpool South terminated at Preston, although on Sundays alternate trains were advertised through to Colne.

January 1955

Table 160 — MANCHESTER, CHORLEY, PRESTON — Week Days

In the late 2010s innovative plans were formulated by open-access company Grand Central (operator of services between London King's Cross, Bradford and Sunderland) for a Blackpool North to London Euston service starting autumn 2020. Staff training and route learning commenced in early 2020 using class 90s, Mark 4 coaches and driving vehicle trailers, with some stock being refurbished and reliveried in the distinctive Grand Central black and orange colours. Regrettably the Covid-19 pandemic and the subsequent downturn in passenger numbers using rail transport, rendered these ambitious plans uneconomic. The scheme was officially abandoned in October 2020.

June 1963

Table 140—
continued FLEETWOOD AND BLACKPOOL TO PRESTON, BOLTON AND MANCHESTER

SATURDAYS ONLY — continued

	p.m.	p.m.	p.m.	p.m.	p.m.	p.m.	p.m.	p.m.	p.m.	p.m.	p.m.	p.m.	p.m.	p.m.	p.m.	p.m.	p.m.	p.m.	p.m.
FLEETWOOD ...dep	...	12V45	1V25	1V25	...	2P10	...	...	2 40	...	...	1V25	2 V5	...	...	...	...	...	
Wyre Dock dep	..	12V47	1V28	1V28	..	2P12	...	...	2 42	...	..	1V28	2 V7	...	..				
Burn Naze	..	12V52	1V33	1V33	..		...	...	2 50	...	..	1V33	2V12	...	..				
Thornton—Cleveleys	..	12V56	1V36	1V36	..	2P24	...	...	2 54	...	..	1V36	2V15	...	...				
BLACKPOOL North ZZ ...dep	..	2 5	2 10	2 20			2 30	2 40			..	2 45	2 57		...				
Layton (Lancs.)	...							2 43							...				
Poulton-le-Fylde ... arr	...					2P29	2 37	2 48	2 59						...				
Poulton-le-Fylde dep						2 44			3 0										
BLACKPOOL Central† ...dep	2 0				2 32		...			2 45		3 15	3 20						4 0
BLACKPOOL South†	2 4				2 35		...			2 51		3 19	3 24						4 4
Squires Gate†	2 8						...					3 22	3 28						4 8
St. Annes-on-the-Sea†	2 13						...					3 26	3 34						4 13
Ansdell and Fairhaven†	2 17						...					3 29	3 38						4 17
Lytham†	2 23						...					3 32	3 44						4 22
Kirkham and Wesham arr	2 34			2 45			...	3 10				3 40	3 54						4 32
Kirkham and Wesham dep	2 35			2 46				3 12				3 40	3 57						4 33
Salwick																			
PRESTON arr	2 47			2 59	3 5			3 28				3 52	4 9						4 45
50 LONDON Euston arr	7 40				8 33														
PRESTON dep	2 53				3 9					3 45		4 15	4 22	4 41	4 45	4 49			
Leyland					3 16							4 22	4 30	...	4 52				
Chorley					3 28							4 36			5 2				
Adlington (Lancs.)															5 8				
Blackrod															5 12				
Lostock Junction															5 18				
Bolton Trinity Street arr					3 46							4 54		5½12	5 25				
Salford arr	3 41				4 8							5 26			5 56				
MANCHESTER Exchange																5 57			
MANCHESTER Victoria	3 45				4 12					4 28		5 30		5 33	6 0				

SATURDAYS ONLY — contd

	p.m.	p.m.	p.m.	p.m.	p.m.	p.m.	p.m.	p.m.	p.m.	p.m.	p.m.	p.m.	p.m.	p.m.	p.m.	p.m.	p.m.	p.m.	p.m.
FLEETWOOD ...dep	..	4 10	...	...	..	...	4 55	...	...	..	...	5 52	...	..	...	...	...	...	
Wyre Dock	..	4 13	...	...	..	...	4 57	...	...	..	...	5 55	...	..	...				
Burn Naze	..	4 18	...	...	..	...	5 2	...	...	..	...	6 1	...	..	...				
Thornton—Cleveleys	..	4 21	...	...	..	...	5 8	...	...	..	...	6 3	...	..	...				
BLACKPOOL North † ZZ ...dep		4 25	...	...	..	...	5 10	...	..	..	5 45	...		..	...	...			
Layton (Lancs.)		4 28	...			...	5 13				5 48				...				
Poulton-le-Fylde arr	4 25	4 33	...			...	5 13	5 19			5 53	6 8			...				
Poulton-le-Fylde dep		4 34	...				5 26					6 9			...				
BLACKPOOL Central† ...dep	4 27		...	4 35		...	5 5	5 24		5 5		6 19		...	6 30		7 5		
BLACKPOOL South†	4 30			4 39		...	5 10	5 28		5 10		6 23		...	6 35		7 9		
Squires Gate†				4 43		...		5 31		5 20		6 26		...	6 39		7 13		
St. Annes-on-the-Sea†				4 48		...		5 35		5 24		6 30		...	6 46		7 18		
Ansdell and Fairhaven†				4 51		...		5 38		5 30		6 33		...	6 50		7 22		
Lytham†				4 57		...		5 41				6 36		...	6 57		7 28		
Kirkham and Wesham arr	4 40	4 44		5 7		...	5 36			5 49		6 19	6 44		...		7 33		
Kirkham and Wesham dep	4 40	4 45		5 8		...	5 37			5 49		6 44			...		7 39		
Salwick		4 49		5 13											7 1½		7 45		
PRESTON arr	4 52	4 58		5 26		...	5 49		5 55	6 0		6 55			...		7 51		
50 LONDON Euston arr		9 57		9 57		...	11 15		11 15						...				
PRESTON dep		5 10	5 27		5 40	5 56					6 44			7 6	7 10	7 19	7 2½	8 6	
Leyland		5 17	...		5 48	6 3								7 7	7 18	...		8 15	
Chorley		5 26	...			6 17								7 21			7 42	8 27	
Adlington (Lancs.)		5 32	...											7 27					
Blackrod		5 37	...											7 31			8 36		
Lostock Junction		5 43	...											7 38					
Bolton Trinity Street arr		5 50				6 35					7½17			7 45			8 1	8 47	
Salford arr		6Z18				6 57								8 17		8 6			
MANCHESTER Exchange		6Z21	6 15				7 1				7 37			8 21		8 10	8 26		

1. Preston to Blackpool Central

PRESTON

II. The 1968 map details the approaches to the station from the south across the River Ribble, the former East Lancashire Railway tracks on the right running almost parallel with the West Coast main line. The line providing access to Preston Docks diverges to the left of the station (see our *Bolton to Preston* album). Preston engine shed is north of the station by Fylde Junction, our route exiting top left away from the line towards Lancaster. The railway shown branching off to the east by the engine shed went to Longridge.

↓ 1. We begin our journey to the Fylde coast on the approach road to the main entrance from Fishergate, Preston's main thoroughfare. The impressive yellow brick building has stood proud since erected by the North Union Railway in 1879. In this picture from 3rd July 2013, as taxis await custom from returning passengers, the supporting metalwork for the electric wiring above the platforms can be seen on the left. There is a second entrance on Butler Street a little further to the left. (Tom Heavyside)

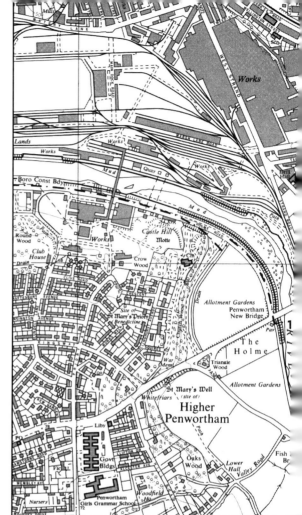

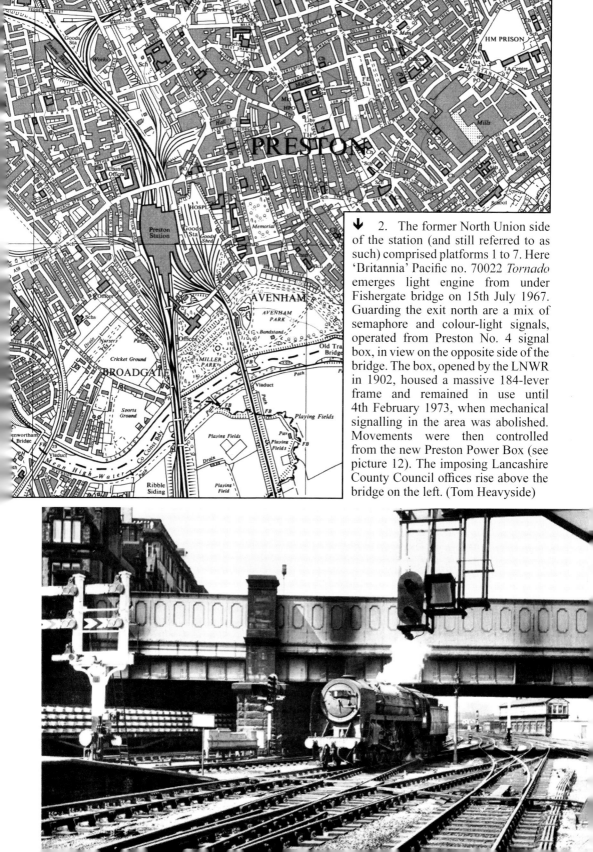

2. The former North Union side of the station (and still referred to as such) comprised platforms 1 to 7. Here 'Britannia' Pacific no. 70022 *Tornado* emerges light engine from under Fishergate bridge on 15th July 1967. Guarding the exit north are a mix of semaphore and colour-light signals, operated from Preston No. 4 signal box, in view on the opposite side of the bridge. The box, opened by the LNWR in 1902, housed a massive 184-lever frame and remained in use until 4th February 1973, when mechanical signalling in the area was abolished. Movements were then controlled from the new Preston Power Box (see picture 12). The imposing Lancashire County Council offices rise above the bridge on the left. (Tom Heavyside)

3. Carnforth-allocated (10A) 'Black 5' 4-6-0 no. 45001 has arrived at platform 13, by the west elevation of Butler Street goods shed on what was formerly the East Lancashire Railway side of the station, with the summer dated 17.45 Windermere-Blackpool service on 3rd August 1967. It will depart south on a five-mile circular detour via Lostock Hall before passing through the station a second time – this time northbound on the North Union side. With no direct connection from the north to the coast lines, this trip around the southern outskirts of Preston obviated the inconvenience of otherwise having to reverse direction in the station. Since the autumn of 1972, following the closure of the ex-East Lancashire lines, there has been no alternative but to change direction within the station environs. The roof above the ex-North Union platforms can be seen on the left. (Tom Heavyside)

4. Locally-based at Lostock Hall shed, 'Black 5' no. 45149 has just been attached to the rear coaches of the 17.05 from London Euston at platform 5, and will shortly leave for Blackpool South, the front portion having already left for Glasgow on 6th April 1968. This proved one of the last regular steam-hauled passenger services on BR before the demise of steam in August. Parcels and mailbags abound by the main platform buildings. The loco was withdrawn two months later in June 1968. (Tom Heavyside)

5. Five years later on 24th March 1973, the overhead wiring is in place ready for the commencement of electric traction south along the West Coast main line the following July. Here Type 4 diesel-electric loco no. 1558 (later no. 47442), built by BR at Crewe Works in February 1964, is ready to depart from the same platform as no. 45149 in the previous picture, with the 15.58 service from London Euston to Blackpool North. The front portion of the train had left for Barrow-in-Furness a few minutes earlier. The platform had been renumbered 3 under the station rationalisation scheme, implemented during the early 1970s. Mail and parcels were still a feature on the platforms, but now mainly stacked in high-sided 'Brutes' (British Rail Universal Trolley Equipment) which could be wheeled easily on and off stopping trains, rather than loosely loaded on trolleys that needed much manhandling, as depicted in 1968. It is now many years since mailbags littered the platforms. (Tom Heavyside)

6. Diesel multiple-units (DMUs) have been running across the Fylde since the late 1950s. Despite the destination blind above the near driving cab stating 'Blackpool', this Birmingham Railway Carriage & Wagon Company-built class 104 three-car set is leaving platform 2 (the former no. 4) southbound for Manchester Victoria on 14th April 1973. The white stripe along the body sides indicated it was one of 13 sets fitted with improved springing during the early 1970s, to allow faster running on the Manchester to Blackpool route. The vehicle on the left is driving trailer composite class 108 no. M56262, the 12 first class seats being behind the driving compartment, their position indicated by the yellow stripe near the roof line, with 53 second class seats located to the left of the door. It was a product of Derby Works in 1959. (Tom Heavyside)

↓   7. While the overhead wires have been in place since 1973, it was not until May 2018 that electric trains were able to proceed to Blackpool. Meanwhile 'Proud Preston' had been accorded city status in 2002. Here four-car unit no. 319382, formerly operated by First Capital Connect on Thameslink services, departs from platform 1 (formerly no. 3) and heads for Blackpool North with a train from Liverpool Lime Street on 6th July 2018. On the right is the old no. 2 platform, which has not been in regular use for passenger services since the early 1970s. (Tom Heavyside)

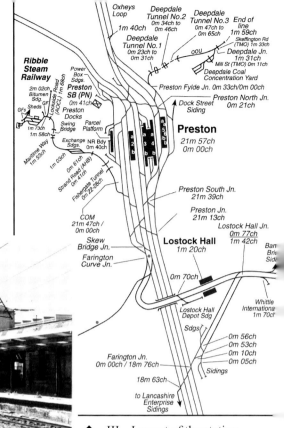

↑   III. Layout of the station and the lines north to Fylde Junction as of 2017.
(© TRACKmaps/ Platform 5 Publishing)

NORTH OF PRESTON

↙ *(bottom left)* 8. Class 8F 2-8-0 no. 48423 draws a mixed freight, mainly coal bound for Wyre Dock at Fleetwood, under this magnificent signal gantry just north of the station on 17th April 1968. The gantry supported no less than 32 signal arms; the stop signals in respect of movements in either direction could effectively only be cleared after being pulled off in both Preston Nos 4 and 5 signal boxes. This was achieved by means of a slot bar and balance weights at the foot of the supporting signal posts, a system known as 'slotting'. No. 5 box, 389 yards north of No. 4, was a similarly designed LNWR box to the latter (see picture 2) housing 126 levers. On the ground are a couple of disc signals used in conjunction with shunting moves. (Ian Simpson)

Preston Engine Shed

9. Regular use of the former LNWR Preston shed ended on 12th September 1961, following a disastrous fire the previous year on 28th June. During its last days it was coded 24K, having been amended from 10B in February 1958. No less than 17 of the 34 steam locos allocated to the shed at the time of the fire had a 4-6-0 wheel arrangement, made up of six 'Black 5s', one 'Patriot' no. 45542, three 'Jubilees' and seven 'Royal Scots'. The latter had only arrived the previous autumn, while two of the 'Jubilees' nos 45582 *Central Provinces* and 45633 *Aden* were very familiar to the local spotting fraternity, having been on the books since 1952 and 1951 respectively. The rest of the stock consisted of two 2P 4-4-0s, four 6P5F 2-6-0s of the Stanier variety, 0F 0-4-0ST no. 47008, five 'Jinty' 0-6-0Ts, three ex-LNWR 7F 0-8-0s and two BR Standard class 2 2-6-0s. Six 0-6-0 diesel shunters (later class 08) were also available to the shed foreman. After the shed's closure the premises were used to store of out-of-service and withdrawn locos. Here brand-new Horwich-built diesel shunter no. D4128 (later no. 08898) draws a couple of unrebuilt 'Patriot' class 4-6-0s, nos 45543 *Home Guard* and unnamed 45550, from the devasted building on 2nd May 1962. The pair were being returned to traffic for the summer after winter storage. Other members of the class can be seen on the left-hand roads: the unrebuilt 'Patriots' were all withdrawn by the end of the year. The early decorative Gothic-style St Walburge's Roman Catholic church, with its slender limestone spire soaring 309 feet skywards, dominates the area. (Bill Ashcroft/John Sloane coll.)

10.   On 22nd September 1963 two withdrawn 0-8-0s nos 49104 and 49408, both dating from LNWR days, built in 1910 and 1922 respectively, stand within the roofless charred remains of the depot awaiting final disposal. In October of the previous year no less than 14 of these veterans were assembled here pending sale for scrap. (RCTS coll.)

11.   During the summer of 1963 the derelict shed is seen from the front carriage of a train about to take the line towards Blackpool. Present by the left-hand wall are nos 49104 and 49408 seen in the previous picture, while nearer the camera a small contingent of 'Patriot' class 4-6-0s await their fate. The redundant coaling tower overlooks the scene on the left.
(M.Moone/Kidderminster Railway Museum coll.)

Fylde Junction

12.   Seen from high on the steeple of St Walburge's church, a class 150 'Sprinter' unit passes below on its way to Blackpool on 24th July 2009. The West Coast main line diverges north towards Lancaster on the left. Preston power signal box, built on the site of Preston shed, which gained control of the area from the former manual boxes on 4th February 1973, is to the right of the stabled unit. Lancashire County Council offices and Fishergate bridge are in the middle distance (see picture 2), with the West Pennine Moors rising beyond. (Tom Heavyside)

WEST OF FYLDE JUNCTION

13. The splendid spire of St Walburge's church looks down on 'Peak' class no. 46025 as it nears Maudland Viaduct with the 07.25 from Newcastle to Blackpool North on Saturday 25th August 1984. The vacated trackbed of the former fast lines between here and Kirkham South Junction, taken out of use on 14th November 1965, can be seen on the left. Derby Works built 56 of these Type 4 locomotives, originally numbered D138 to D193 and later designated class 46, between October 1961 and January 1963. They had Sulzer engines rated at 2,500hp, a 1Co-Co1 wheel arrangement, turned the scales at 138 tons and had a top speed of 90mph. Latterly no. 46025 had led a charmed existence inasmuch as it was withdrawn in December 1980, only to be reinstated in November 1981. It survived a further three months after this photograph was exposed. (Tom Heavyside)

14. The last surviving 'Britannia' 4-6-2 on BR's books, no. 70013 *Oliver Cromwell*, creeps by Maudland Viaduct signal box with the Railway Correspondence & Travel Society 'Lancastrian No. 2 Railtour' en route from Fleetwood to Windermere on 20th April 1968. The rear coaches are straggling the 10-arch viaduct. The all-timber constructed signal box enclosing a 42-lever frame had stood in this seemingly precarious position since 1889: it became defunct when its functions were taken over by Preston power box in February 1973. (Tom Heavyside)

15. The signalman's view of Rose Grove (Burnley)-based class 8F 2-8-0 no. 48423, as it plods towards Preston with a pick-up goods from the Fylde on 7th March 1968. Terraced rows lie below the viaduct, the only such structure on the lines under review, while a former cotton mill is prominent on the right. The loco remained on the books of Rose Grove until the very end of regular steam traction on BR in August 1968. (Ian Simpson)

EAST OF SALWICK

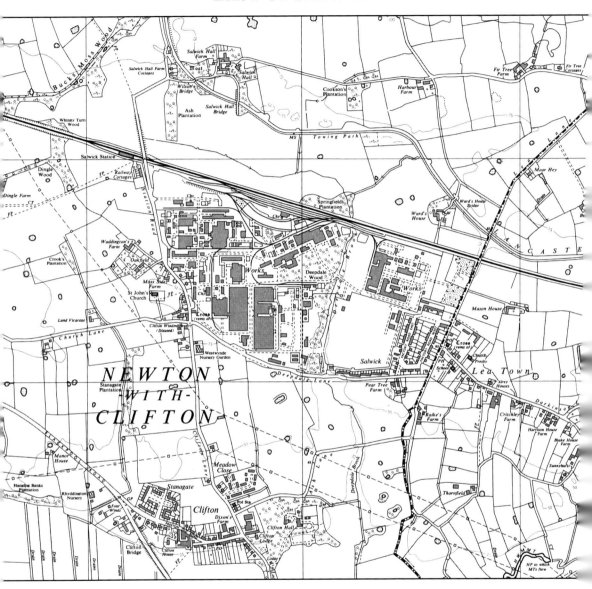

IV. This 1965 extract of the Salwick area highlights the land taken over by the Royal Ordnance for its Springfields factory, and the internal railway system developed during the early years of World War II. Salwick station is near the left-hand edge, while Lea Road water troughs ran beneath the lane on the right, close by the Lancaster Canal. The canal was cut in the 1790s and remained in use for the carriage of goods until 1947; today only pleasure barges negotiate its waters. A mile or so to the east of here, planning permission was granted in November 2022 for a new station, virtually on the same site as the May 1938 closed Lea Road station, to be known as Cottam Parkway to serve the expanding suburbs of Preston.

16.   Travelling along the down fast line, 2-6-0 no. 42828 passes over Lea Road water troughs with a Blackburn to Blackpool Central train on Saturday 20th July 1963. Commonly referred to as 'Crabs', members of this 245-strong class, built by the LMS between 1926 and 1932 (no. 42828 at Horwich in 1929), were often seen on passenger work on summer weekends. The troughs laid in 1885 were 561 yards long. The Lancaster Canal can be discerned above the smokebox of no. 42828. (Chris Spring)

17.   Turning to face west at Salwick, class 40 no. 393 (later no. 40193) dashes by the site of the former troughs with the summer Saturday 13.32 from Blackpool North to Bradford Exchange and Castleford on 21st July 1973. These heavyweight 1Co-Co1 locomotives (they turned the scales at 133 tons) produced by English Electric from 1958 were regularly employed on such trains. Nearer the camera the trackbed of the former fast lines is clearly visible. The extent of the Springfields factory in the background, on the south side of the line, is apparent (see following two pictures). (Tom Heavyside)

Royal Ordnance Springfields Factory

18. Peckett 0-4-0ST works no. 2003 built in 1941 for the Royal Ordnance factory at Swynnerton in Staffordshire, was based here for some 25 years from 1946. It was photographed on 31st May 1959. Today the loco is housed at the Ribble Steam Railway at Preston – see our *Bolton to Preston* album. (Jim Peden photograph/ copyright Industrial Railway Society)

19. Another long-term resident at Springfields was Hudswell Clarke 0-4-0 diesel-mechanical loco works no. D628, which arrived new from the maker's Leeds factory in 1943. Rail traffic ceased in December 1991, the site then being owned by British Nuclear Fuels, the loco subsequently being cared for by a works preservation society. It is seen outside the brick-built shed on 9th October 1993. Partially visible is the Hudswell Clarke trade mark steam age chimney used to exhaust the spent gases. Currently the loco is again a companion of the Peckett loco seen in the previous picture, having also moved to the Ribble Steam Railway, where it rejoices with the name *Mighty Atom*. The factory is now operated by Springfields Fuels Ltd. (Adrian Booth)

20. Class 46 no. 46026 *Leicestershire & Derbyshire Yeomanry* (no. D163 when new from Derby Works in April 1962), rushes by Salwick No. 2 (officially plain Salwick from November 1975) signal box at the approach to the station, with a summer dated train bound for Blackpool North on Saturday 2nd July 1983. The box, which latterly housed a 35-lever frame, became a fringe box to Preston power box in February 1973; Salwick No. 1 signal box, which opened in 1942 to facilitate a connection to the Springfields factory at the east end of the site, was closed at the same time. It was located by the trees in the middle distance. There has obviously been much track rational-isation on the right, the remaining siding serving the Springfields factory can be discerned by the fifth carriage. Salwick signal box, along with all the remaining manual boxes on the Fylde, became defunct at the start of the electrification work in November 2017, with movements on completion supervised from the Manchester Rail Operating Centre. East of Salwick Preston Power Box retains control for the time being. (Tom Heavyside)

SALWICK

21. Opened early 1842 as Salwick Road with the suffix dropped from June of that year. Closed by the LMS on 2nd May 1938, its island platform was reopened during the early days of World War II, principally for the benefit of workers at the Springfields factory. It became unstaffed from 18th January 1971. A diesel multiple-unit formation consisting of four cars displaying mixed liveries, heads away from the camera towards the coast on the same day as the previous picture. Presumably the rear unit had visited Irlam a little earlier! The platform buildings were removed during the mid-1970s, leaving the canopy supported by decorative iron columns to offer some comfort to waiting passengers at this exposed and somewhat isolated location. In 1983 only three westbound and two trains in the opposite direction were timetabled to call here. (Tom Heavyside)

22. On 1st September 1984 the station had a rather untended look, with grasses and weeds proliferating on the west end of the platform, as class 45 no. 45126 races by with the Saturdays only summer dated 13.40 from Blackpool North to York service. The loco was originally numbered D32 when completed at Derby Works in June 1961. It was withdrawn in April 1987. (Tom Heavyside)

23. The refurbished station looks quite pristine following the electrification work in 2018. A Virgin Trains West Coast five-car class 221 'Super Voyager' hurries towards Blackpool with the 16.33 from London Euston on 11th June of that year. These Bombardier units were first introduced in 2001, and with a Cummins 750hp engine underslung beneath each vehicle, providing a total 3750hp, are able to travel at up to 125mph. The road bridge was one of 11 on the Fylde that had to be reconstructed to accommodate the overhead wires. Note there is still room on the north side for a pair of fast lines to pass below, should they ever be relaid! Today, on weekdays three trains stop in each direction but none on Sundays. (Tom Heavyside)

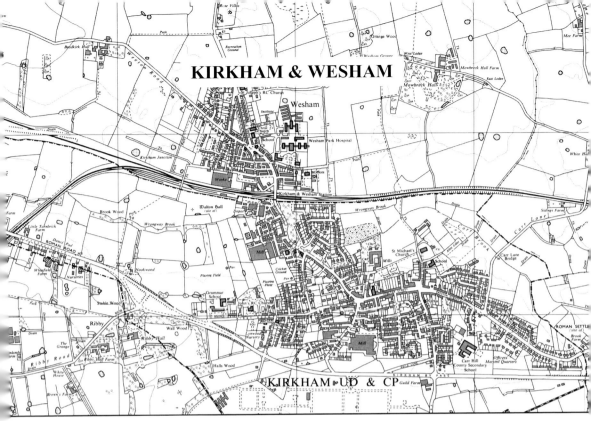

KIRKHAM & WESHAM

V. The station is located in Wesham, inhabited by 3,584 souls in 2011, while 7,194 lived across the border in Kirkham. The layout depicted here dated from the quadrupling of the line from Preston in 1888-89, the original stopping place, known simply as Kirkham, being a short way to the west of the present station. Wesham was added to the title in the mid-1900s. West of the station the divergence of the line to Blackpool Central via St Annes from that to Blackpool North and Fleetwood is noted as Kirkham Junction. The signal box also controlled the direct Marton line to Blackpool South (see picture 31), but this has not been recorded.

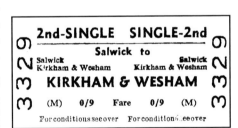

24. The entrance to the booking hall was pictured on 29th April 2015. It is an archetypical yellow-brick, hipped-roofed Lancashire & Yorkshire Railway building, that apart from the signs, poster boards, telephone kiosk and lighting has changed little since its construction in 1889. The red rose symbol below the double-arrow logo on the station sign, is a vivid reminder that this is Lancashire County Council territory. (Tom Heavyside)

25.   Moving downstairs to the island platform during the summer of 1963, class 5 no. 45233 stops while heading east from Blackpool. The engine was a product of Armstrong Whitworth in August 1936, one of 327 built by the Newcastle company for the LMS. The 4-6-0 was a long-standing resident of Newton Heath shed, Manchester, having been based there since June 1938. Suggs gas lamps were lit during the hours of darkness. (Peter Ward/RCTS coll.)

26.   The following year on 13th June 1964, a much younger 'Black 5' no. 44725, released from Crewe Works in April 1949, rushes by on the down fast line with train reporting number 1P30, a summer Saturday relief service from Manchester Victoria. Destined for Blackpool North, it has a clear road ahead through Kirkham North Junction, as indicated by the pulled off distant signal above the leading carriage. In the foreground are crossovers between the up slow and loop lines. The semaphore signals in the distance are near Kirkham South Junction. The billboards on the left advertise some of the attractions to be had at Blackpool that summer, including artists Mike and Bernie Winters and a reminder to visit the Pleasure Beach. (Chris Spring)

27.   Young admirers watch class 25s nos 7601 and 7607 pass with returning passengers from Blackpool North to Scotland on 21st July 1973. Both locos were products of Derby Works in 1966, being renumbered 25251 and 25257 respectively in April 1974. In the intervening period since the previous picture, the platform canopies had been removed, as had the up loop line on the right. Sandwiched between the up and down fast lines is the 54-lever Kirkham Station signal box. It had taken over the functions of Kirkham South Junction in June 1968; in turn it was abolished in November 1975 when Kirkham North Junction took command of the locality. Lighting is now by electricity rather than gas. (Tom Heavyside)

28.   We can now examine the south side of the platform buildings as passengers alighted from five months old 'Pacer' no. 142045, forming the 15.34 Ormskirk to Blackpool South service, make their way towards the exit on 2nd August 1986. The unit is finished in Provincial sector two-tone blue livery. Posters extolling the benefits of railcards flank the chargeman's office, while tickets could be obtained in the comfort of the waiting room further along the platform. Over two years from May 1985 96 of these two-car class 142 units entered service. The bodies, essentially an adapted bus design, were manufactured by Leyland National at Workington, before final assembly on a four-wheeled chassis at British Rail Engineering at Derby. The class was destined to be the mainstay of services along the coast line for over 30 years. Since their banishment from the main lines in 2020, no less than 35 142s have been given a new lease of life at a number of heritage railways or at various sites for community use, no. 142045 being donated to Kirk Merrington Primary School, near Spennymoor, County Durham in October 2020. (Tom Heavyside)

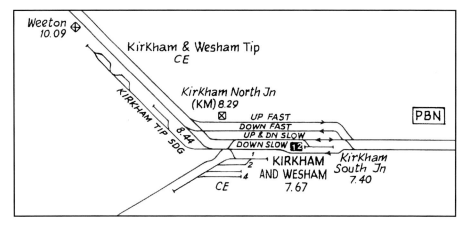

VI. Layout at Kirkham & Wesham in 1990. (©TRACKmaps)

29. The class 142s were refurbished between 1998 and 2002 when Cummins engines rated at 230hp replaced the original Leyland 205hp engines. With the fast lines on the left, no. 142058 leaves platform 2 with a train from Blackpool South to Colne, as a fellow 'Pacer' departs from platform 1 in the opposite direction on 23rd June 2015. Both units display the distinctive dark blue and mauve livery adopted by Northern Rail. The section of the building nearest the camera in the previous picture has made way for a horticultural area, a more basic waiting shelter being provided instead of the former waiting room. Some wag has turned the 'Way Out' sign to point away from the covered stairway leading to the exit. Tickets are again purchased from the old road level booking office. The fast and slow lines converge between the trees in the middle distance at Kirkham South Junction. No. 142058 is also among the surviving 'Pacers', having found a new home at the Telford Steam Railway, Shropshire. (Tom Heavyside)

30. The station was closed temporarily for electrification work on 11th November 2017, reopening for trains to Blackpool South on 29th January 2018. Blackpool North services recommenced on 20th May. The revamped station and layout included a new up line and platform 3 on the north side, the installation of lifts to allow easy access to the platforms for the less nimble and a new footbridge, the large letters inscribed on its panels leaving little doubt as to the location. Platform 1 to the left of the amenity block has been retained but not electrified, and is available for trains to Blackpool South only. The former fast lines, which were behind the fence on the right, have been lifted. Here on 17th September 2021, with pantographs raised CAF 'Civity' nos. 331010 and 331011 roll alongside platform 3 with the 10.57 service from Blackpool North to Manchester Airport, as an Avanti West Coast class 390 'Pendolino' from London Euston disappears in the opposite direction. 31 of these three-car CAF units entered service from July 2019, after importation from the builder's Zaragoza factory in Spain. From a station stop they are able to reach a speed of 77mph in 45 seconds, and sustain a maximum 100mph. (Tom Heavyside)

WEST OF KIRKHAM & WESHAM

Kirkham North Junction

↓ 31. The intricate trackwork at this three-way junction can be studied in this panorama from Saturday 29th August 1964. The signal box dating from 1903 contained a 105-lever frame. Eastbound is a rather decrepit-looking Caprotti valve gear-fitted 'Black 5' no. 44749 in charge of the 2.57pm from Blackpool North to Sheffield Victoria. The engine would be relieved in the Manchester area by an electric locomotive for the journey across the Pennines via the Woodhead route. The line descending towards the signal box, behind the sixth carriage, is the up passenger loop off the direct Marton route from Blackpool South, which crossed the Poulton lines by the flyover seen in the distance. The lines to Blackpool Central via the coast veer off to the left. This was probably the last trip to the seaside for this 4-6-0 as it was withdrawn the following week after a comparatively short life of 12 years. (Ron Herbert)

→ 32. On the same day as the previous picture, looking east towards Kirkham station which can be seen in the background, five-year-old English Electric Type 4 no. D224 *Lucania* was recorded on the down fast line with the 11.00am from London Euston to Blackpool Central. The train was scheduled to call at all stations between Lytham and its destination, the raised semaphore on the right-hand post confirming its routing via the coast line. The tall chimney pointing skyward once served the Phoenix cotton mill. The loco, named after a former Cunard ocean liner, was withdrawn as no. 40024 in June 1984. (Ron Herbert)

→ 33. A two-car Derby class 108 diesel multiple-unit leads a Birmingham Railway Carriage & Wagon Company three-car class 104 set past the same spot as the previous photograph, while forming a Manchester Victoria to Blackpool North service on 12th July 1975. First class accommodation was available as shown by the yellow bands near the roof lines. As indicated by the remaining signal arm on the left-hand post, if directed onto the fast line at Kirkham South Junction trains could then only continue in the Poulton direction, the connections to the coast line having been removed in the spring of 1972. The siding seen to the left of no. D224 in picture 32 had also been dispensed with. More semaphores can be discerned near the station. (Tom Heavyside)

34. No. 37031 hurries by the simplified layout on the up fast with the 12.40 Blackpool North to Sheffield service on 1st September 1984. The slow and fast lines merge beyond the signal box, and the points allowing access to the remaining stub of the Marton line (see picture 63) can also be seen. The single lead onto the coast line and the engineers sidings are on the left. The class 37 left the English Electric's Vulcan Foundry at Newton-le-Willows in Lancashire as no. D6731 in October 1961, being declared surplus to requirements by BR in January 1994. Note the front-end connecting doors and the blanked-off split headcode boxes. (Tom Heavyside)

35. The junction was again remodelled during the electrification work. A couple of two-car 'Sprinter' units, with no. 150214 at the rear, head towards Blackpool South with the 11.57 from Preston on 13th April 2019. The long single line section through to Blackpool South, and worked on the one engine in steam principle, commences behind the trees on the left. Trains from the coast now join the down line to Blackpool North (bottom right), before almost immediately crossing to the up line. The picture was taken from the late 1990s constructed A585 bypass road, the signal box prior to demolition being almost below the new bridge. Little remains of the former engineers sidings. (Tom Heavyside)

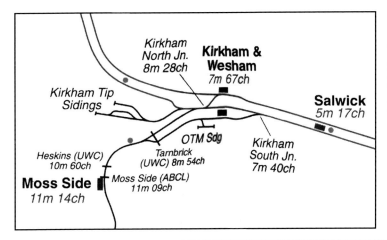

VII. Layout of the remodelled junction pending electrification. (© TRACKmaps/ Platform 5 Publishing)

WREA GREEN

VIII. The station opened as Wray Green in 1846. Running-in boards etc were amended when this up-market village was renamed Wrea Green in August 1875 to avoid confusion with Wray, near Hornby east of Carnforth, following a campaign by the local vicar. Scattered around what is the largest village green in Lancashire was a population of 401 in 1891: this had increased to 1,464 in 1981. The original path of the Preston & Wyre Railway is evident east of the station, this becoming defunct when the current line from Kirkham opened in 1874, although for a time a short section was maintained as a siding. This extract is from 1955.

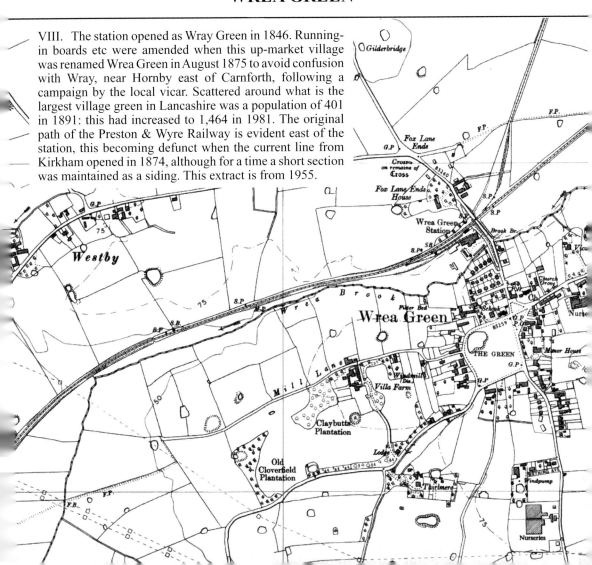

36.   One of the rather ungainly looking 'Black 5s' no. 44745, one of 22 fitted with Caprotti valve gear, passes non-stop en route to Blackpool Central on a rather hazy Sunday 25th June 1961. A mineral wagon stands on the line leading to the small goods yard, while Brook Corn Mill on the far right of the frame was served by a separate siding. The station closed the next day. (Chris Spring)

37.   In the opposite direction on a bitterly cold 26th January 1963, 4-6-0 no. 45574 *India*, one of Blackpool's long-serving 'Jubilees', where it had been shedded since July 1937, dashes by bound for Manchester Victoria. From this position we can study the trackwork giving access to the goods yard and corn mill siding, although the post and bracket from which formerly hung a loading gauge, then served little purpose! The cameraman has his back to the 16-lever signal box, which was closed on 12th September 1965, the goods yard having ceased business the previous month. *India* left its seaside home of 27 years when transferred to Carlisle Kingmoor in September 1964: it was subsequently withdrawn from Leeds Holbeck shed in March 1966. Today there is no evidence a station ever existed here, the goods shed also having been demolished, while the small Brook Mill Industrial Estate occupies the old corn mill site. Desires to reopen the station remain unfulfilled. (Chris Spring)

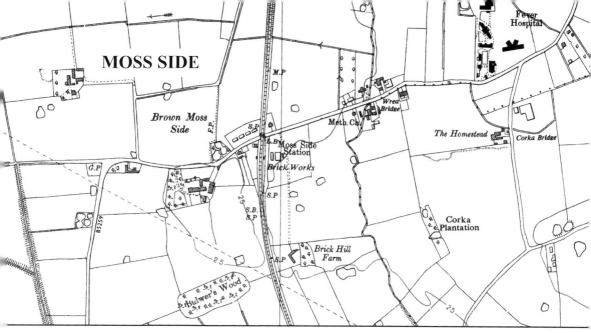

IX.   The station occupies a quiet spot by a country lane. The adjacent brickworks is now long-closed. This 6ins to the mile map is dated 1955.

38.   In its last months of service, having taken over from a diesel locomotive at Preston, no. 42105 rushes over the level crossing towards the closed platforms (the last train called on 25th June 1961), with the 09.05 London Euston to Blackpool South service in September 1966. The large wheel used to close and open the crossing gates is visible behind the signal box windows. The need for the 16-lever box, which had stood watching over the B5269 Kirkham to Lytham road since 1876, ended on 30th March 1983 following the installation of automatic barriers. No. 42105 was a Fairburn variant of the LMS 2-6-4Ts, and was among a batch of 41 constructed by BR at Brighton Works for the Southern Region during 1950 and 1951. After working from Tunbridge Wells West, Exmouth Junction and Brighton sheds, it moved to the London Midland Region in December 1959, serving its last days from October 1965 attached to Lostock Hall shed, Preston. It was condemned in December 1966. (Peter Fitton/Colour-Rail.com)

39.   The station was reopened when the old up platform was reinstated on 21st November 1983, coinciding with the singling of the line between Kirkham and St Annes. Only a basic 'bus shelter' was provided for passengers' needs. The poster proclaimed the advent of the 'Pacers', with 'new comfortable coaching stock', along with direct services to Preston from 12th May 1986. Here seven-months old 'Pacer' no. 142034 leaves for the coast with the 16.52 service from Ormskirk on 2nd August 1986. (Tom Heavyside)

40.   'Sprinter' no 150144 recedes from the camera with 18.22 departure from Blackpool South to Colne on 17th May 2018. Drivers are still required to 'whistle' before proceeding over this level crossing, the only one on the south line. The former down platform remains in place, although somewhat overgrown. (Tom Heavyside)

SOUTH OF MOSS SIDE

Lytham Motive Power Museum

41.   During the late 1960s a varied selection of locomotives, mainly four-coupled saddle tanks, along with a wide range of other railway and transport related artefacts, were assembled for display at business premises along Dock Road, which leads to the shipbuilding yard - by the right-hand edge of map X. Here a visitor looks on with interest at the outside exhibits on 10th August 1969. Nearest the camera is a somewhat clumsy looking 0-4-0ST *Vulcan*, put together at its namesake Vulcan Foundry at Newton-le-Willows, Lancashire in 1932, where for many years it was used as a works shunter. The firebox, boiler and smokebox previously formed part of a narrow gauge loco, which were matched with a larger saddle tank, cab and chimney etc for their new role as components of a standard gauge loco. It now resides at Beamish – the Living Museum of the North, in County Durham. Partly hidden is 2ft gauge loco *Jonathan* of 1898 vintage, transported from Dinorwic Slate Quarries at Llanberis in North Wales two years earlier. It was a product of the Hunslet Engine Company of Leeds. Presently *Jonathan* is back here after visiting a number of preserved railways in the interim. Near the exhibition hall is a traction engine, with ex-LNER Pullman carriage *Minerva* resting beyond the tall semaphore signal on the left.
(T.A. Fletcher/John Marshall coll./Kidderminster Railway Mueum coll.)

42. Previously owned by Ribble Cement at Clitheroe, 0-4-0ST *Ribblesdale No. 3*, manufactured by Hudswell Clarke in 1936, stands in the purpose-built roundhouse on 29th February 1992. This was preview day pending an auction of exhibits the following morning: on the right a platform indicator stand of a type once common on BR was lot 41. (Tom Heavyside)

43. On the same day, facing the camera on the right, crane-tank *Snipey* constructed by Neilson of Glasgow in 1890 and formerly of Hodbarrow Iron Mines, Millom, Cumberland, along with, on the left, an 0-4-0ST built by the North British Locomotive Company of Glasgow in 1908 and onetime of Bairds & Scottish Steel at Gartsherrie, near Coatbridge, await potential buyers. However, at the auction these two locos, along with *Ribblesdale No. 3* seen in the previous picture went unsold. Today they remain stored inside the roundhouse together with other items which failed to attract sufficient bids, although the museum is no longer open to the public. (Tom Heavyside)

Lytham Goods

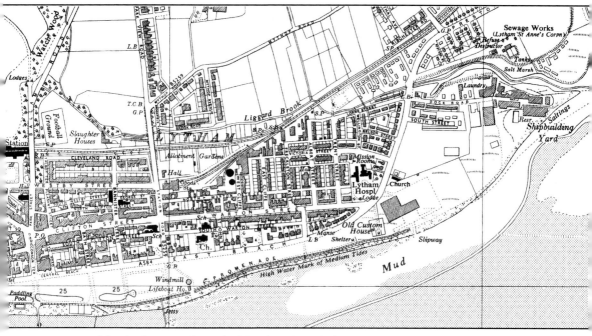

X.   Its position is shown at the end of the short branch from Lytham Goods Junction on this 1955 map. Opened in February 1846 as the Lytham terminus of the erstwhile Preston & Wyre Railway, it enjoyed a relatively short existence as a passenger station, closing on 1st July 1874. From that date trains were able to travel through from Kirkham to Blackpool by way of a connection laid between the former P&W and the ex-Blackpool & Lytham railways. The former station was then retained for goods purposes until 1st April 1963. The branch also served the former Lytham Urban District Council gas works, adjacent to North Warton Street and West Cliffe.

44.   One year after closure, this was the scene looking towards the interior of the shed on 12th April 1964. By this time the former six tracks which ended here had been recovered. The roof over the 140ft long, 53ft wide shed was held aloft by 11 timber-arched trusses.
(John Marshall/Kidderminster Railway Museum coll.)

45. The classical architectural features of the stone façade, overlooking the appropriately named Station Road, stood defiant as to its earlier importance at the entrance to what was a mere goods depot for nearly 90 years. Structurally the building was looking a little neglected when recorded on the same day as the previous picture. With BR having vacated the site it would appear some found it a convenient free parking area – cars include nearest the camera a Morris Oxford, while by the side wall of the main building, flanked by a Hillman Minx and a Triumph Mayflower is a three-wheeled Bond Minicar. The latter were manufactured in Preston from 1948, where production continued until 1966. The billboard on the left advertised a fare to London of 51/9d (£2.58p). After demolition in the mid-1960s the land subseqently became occupied by a Lancashire Fire and Rescue Station. The pub next door dating from 1847, now a Wetherspoon's establishment, still rejoices as 'The Railway Hotel'. (John Marshall/Kidderminster Railway Museum coll.)

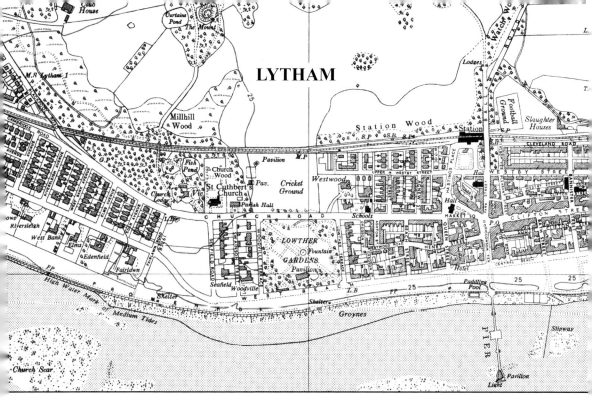

XI.   The former B&LR terminus became available for through traffic to Blackpool from July 1874. It is half-a-mile west of Lytham Goods Junction. From the station forecourt it is a half-mile walk to the sea front. This 6ins to 1 mile map is from 1955.

46.   Framed by the platform canopies and footbridge (new in 1962), class 5 4-6-0 no. 45495 prepares to halt with the 3.20pm from Blackpool Central to Manchester Victoria on 2nd September 1964. The roof of the signal box protrudes above the rear two coaches; its 28-lever frame was in use from 1921, when it replaced a previous box, until 12th October 1971. The bay platform just visible on the left was once frequented by a rail-motor service between here and Blackpool. (A.C.Gilbert/Manchester Locomotive Society coll.)

47.   Derby class 108 twin-unit nos M56224 (leading) and M50976 arrive at the then unstaffed station with the 19.28 service from Blackpool South to Kirkham on 16th August 1980. Alighting passengers had a choice of exit, either up the slope on the right to the main road or over the footbridge to the down platform, part of which has been fenced off. The removal of the canopies had left passengers at the mercy of the elements. (Tom Heavyside)

48.   Six years later, observed from the footbridge, 'Pacer' no 142034 approaches with the 18.30 Blackpool South-Ormskirk service on 2nd August 1986. Only the former down line remained in use after single line working was instigated in November 1983. The area to the left of the former bay platform had been resurfaced to provide car parking facilities. (Tom Heavyside)

49a.   In 1987 the vacated station buildings were extended over part of the down platform and reopened as a pub and restaurant. Here intending passengers look towards 'Pacer' no. 142065 approaching with the 16.15 Blackpool South-Preston service on 9th August 2018. The poster board by the exit advertises some of the gastronomic delights to be had in the adjacent eatery. Floral decorations are maintained by friends of the station, locals also looking after the old up platform which provides a welcome haven for insects and birds. The unit was one of 13 that continued to work on the main lines until the latter half of 2020. (Tom Heavyside)

49b.   The fine frontage of the former station building recorded on 23rd February 2023. The entrance to the platform is on the right. These days the clock above what is now the entrance to the pub is of little use – only showing the correct time twice each day! (Tom Heavyside)

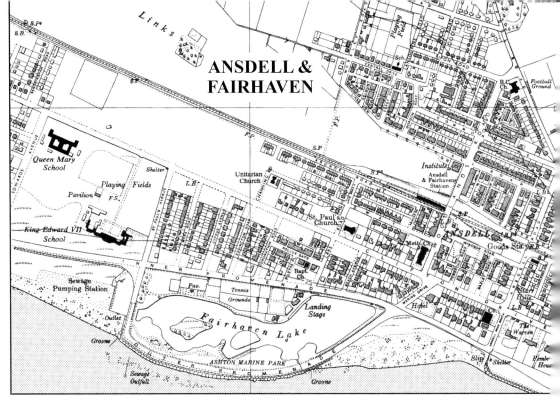

XII. The station and goods yard are either side of Woodland Road on this 1955 map. This stopping place, originally known as Ansdell, opened in October 1903 when it replaced a previous station 370 yards to the east, that had sold its first tickets in 1872. It has been known by its current title since January 1906. Half-a-mile away is the relaxing Fairhaven Lake overlooking the Ribble estuary, from where Southport can be seen some 10 miles away across the water.

50. Blackpool had been home to class 5 4-6-0 no. 45436 since September 1953, here seen pulling away from the station with the five-coach 11.45am service from Blackpool Central to Manchester Victoria on 4th April 1964. The station entrance on Woodland Road rises above the rear coaches. The goods yard on the left appears devoid of wagons; it received its last delivery of coal for distribution by local merchants in August 1965. (Chris Spring)

51. Two days later 'Jubilee' class 4-6-0 no. 45657 *Tyrwhitt* leaves the long island platform while heading the 4.40pm Liverpool Exchange to Blackpool Central service. The station became unmanned in 1971, the signal box on the right containing a 40-lever frame, being switched out permanently on 12th October of that year. The next year the station buildings, including the entrance hall, were reduced to rubble and cleared. (Chris Spring)

52. 'Pacer' no. 142056 prepares to stop at the same platform as *Tyrwhitt* in the previous picture, while returning to Preston on 8th October 2018. A basic shelter now suffices for passengers' needs. The former up side of the platform to the right has been given over to nature. Not evident on this occasion, the station can be very busy when major golf championships, such as 'The Open', are staged at the nearby Royal Lytham & St Annes Golf Club. (Tom Heavyside)

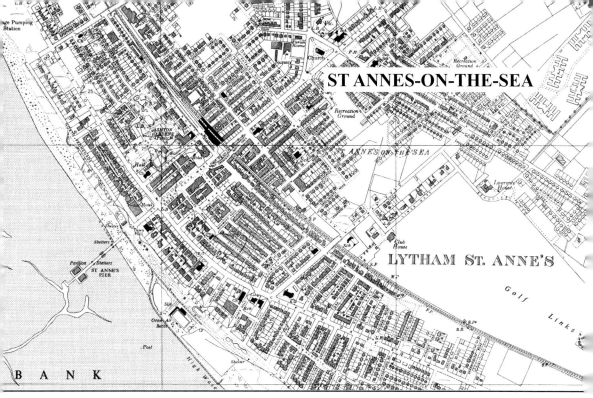

XIII.   The station is half-a-mile inland from the Promenade. West Crescent climbs steeply off St Annes Road West to an overbridge overlooking the platforms. The goods facility lies parallel to St Annes Road North. Although remaining distinct, Lytham and St Annes were joined together as a municipal borough in 1922.

53.   Bank Hall (Liverpool)-allocated no. 75047, a BR Standard class 4 4-6-0, heads for home with the 9.00am stopping service from Blackpool Central to Liverpool Exchange on 13th June 1964. The track had been lifted from the short bay platform on the right, while a 16 ton mineral wagon occupies the goods yard behind the fence on the left. The yard closed on 25th November 1968. The signal box is just visible behind the rear coach. Note the 'St Annes' totem signs attached to the concrete lampposts, although the town's full title was acknowledged in the timetables. No.75047 left Swindon Works new in October 1953 and was withdrawn in August 1967. (Chris Spring)

54. Single line working was introduced beyond St Annes on 8th March 1982. With the severed former up line on the left, a Derby class 108 DMU forming the 17.32 from Kirkham to Blackpool South, leaves the station behind on 18th August 1983. Returning trains from Blackpool used the 15mph speed restricted crossover by the signal box to gain the up line. The box when built in 1923 had a 32-lever frame, which was reduced to 16 in 1965. It continued to be manned until 20th November 1983, when the line between here and Kirkham North Junction was singled. (Noel Machell)

55. From November 1983 only the down platform remained in use. Note the wide expanse of the platforms protected by twin canopies, and the covered footbridge. A hybrid two-car DMU, consisting of vehicles of classes 108 (leading) and 104, call with the 09.24 service from Blackpool South to Kirkham on 28th May 1985. The destination blind appears to be out-of-use. (Noel Machell)

56a.   In 1986 the former commodious facilities were replaced by a much more modest compact building, with little shelter available for waiting passengers in less ideal seaside weather conditions. The width of the platform was reduced considerably, but the station signs now announce the town's full title, St Annes-on-the-Sea. It is the only manned station along the coast line. Here 'Pacer' no. 142046 is about to stop with the 14.38 from Preston to Blackpool South on a scorching 23rd May 2018. Adding to the ambience are the platform planters, looked after by Lytham St Annes Gardening Club, while by way of contrast the former up platform remains untended and rather overgrown. After running its last the 'Pacer' was forwarded to Sims of Newport, South Wales, for scrapping in January 2020. (Tom Heavyside)

56b.   The functional building as seen from the approach road in February 2023. The blue plaque by the station entrance on the left (enlarged, right) extols the tenuous links with the town of the famed LNER Chief Mechanical Engineer, Sir Nigel Gresley, in that he married a local lady at the parish church in October 1901. The Amazon lockers on the right, by the poster case giving information on the South Fylde Line, are a recent addition. (Tom Heavyside)

Pleasure Island

57.   For some eight years from August 1994, strollers along the Promenade at St Annes were able to admire this Peckett of Bristol manufactured 0-4-0ST *Daphne* of 1899 vintage on a short section of track. It was recorded on 29th May 1996. While the carriages remain in situ serving as a cafe and gift shop, the engine is now on the stock list of the Ribble Steam Railway at Preston.
(Tom Heavyside)

SQUIRES GATE

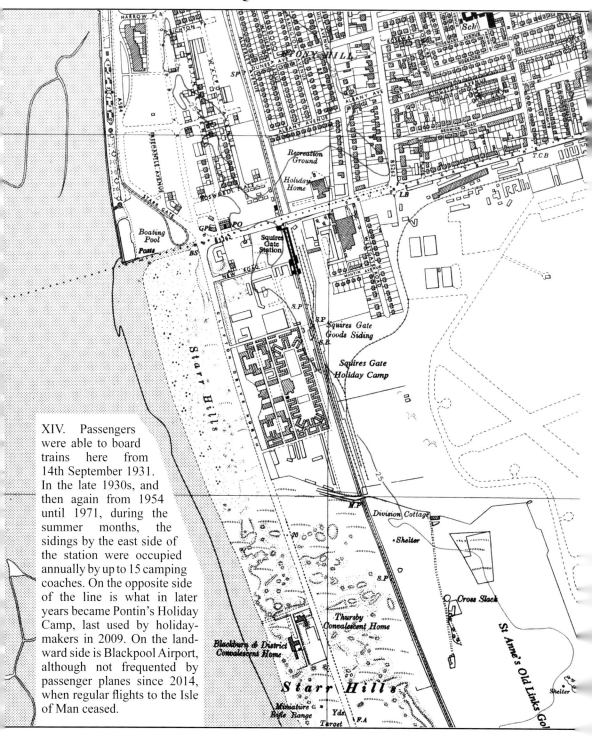

XIV. Passengers were able to board trains here from 14th September 1931. In the late 1930s, and then again from 1954 until 1971, during the summer months, the sidings by the east side of the station were occupied annually by up to 15 camping coaches. On the opposite side of the line is what in later years became Pontin's Holiday Camp, last used by holiday-makers in 2009. On the land-ward side is Blackpool Airport, although not frequented by passenger planes since 2014, when regular flights to the Isle of Man ceased.

58.   In this late 1950s scene, no. 45642 *Boscawen* eases a train from Blackpool Central under the main road bridge. Passengers making their way towards the staircase were reminded to have 'Tickets and Concessions Ready'. In reality this was the pioneer 'Jubilee' class 4-6-0 no. (4)5552 built by the LMS at Crewe Works in May 1934. The loco had exchanged identities with the original no. (4)5642 built in December 1934, when the latter was renumbered as first of class no. 5552, and named *Silver Jubilee* to mark the 25th anniversary of the reign of King George V and Queen Mary in 1935. (H.B.Priestley/Robert Humm coll.)

59.   Observed from the defunct up platform after the line had been singled, the first 'Sprinter' class 150/2 no. 150201, released from British Rail Engineering at York in September 1986, calls with the 09.30 Blackpool South to Colne service on the glorious spring morning of 15th May 1989. The removal of the platform canopies, along with the roofing above the footbridge and steps leading to the former up platform, allows a view of the rather unsalubrious back wall and supporting framework of the roadside station building. Two of the windows have been bricked-up, the office no longer being required by BR after the station became unstaffed, while the section to the left, originally let to a bank, remained in commercial use. The building was not demolished until the late 1990s. (Noel Machell)

60. The guard of the 11.13 from Blackpool South to Preston waits patiently at the far end of 'Pacer' no. 142032 while business is concluded on 8th October 2018. The old up platform, then in a rather woebegone state, has pleasingly since been tidied, with a new fence displaying among other items crests of the L&YR and the LMS. Residents of the recently-erected houses on the site of the former sidings have a grandstand view of passing trains. (Tom Heavyside)

BLACKPOOL PLEASURE BEACH

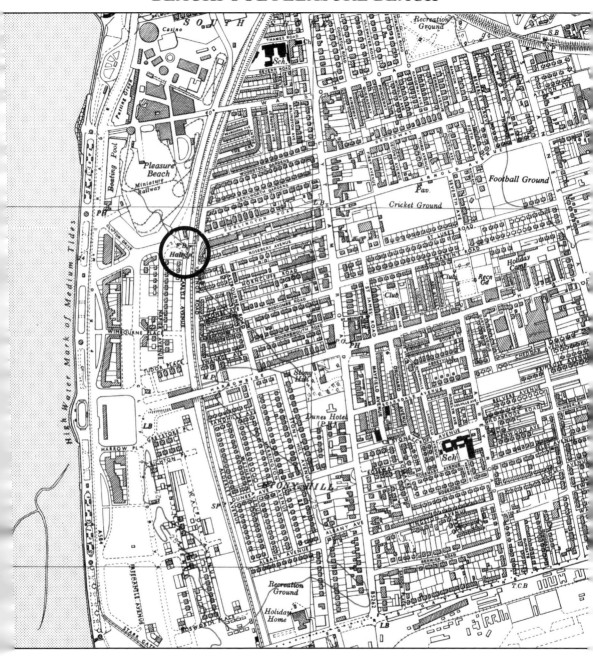

XV.   The revived 13th April 1987 facility (circled), is on the site of the former Burlington Road Halt, initially open for two years from 1st October 1913, then again from 1919 until 11th September 1939. Main beneficiary of the halt was the nearby Pleasure Beach (hence war-time closures). Significantly the miniature railway appears as one of the major attractions.

61.   Another of the ubiquitous 'Black 5' 4-6-0s no. 45377 (in total 842 were built from 1934 with the last in 1951) approaches the site of the future (former) station on 16th May 1964. It is hauling nine coaches forming the 3.20pm from Blackpool Central to Manchester Victoria. The Big Dipper can be seen left, just one of many not for the faint-hearted hair-raising attractions at this renowned fun fair. For those of a more timid disposition, a more conventional 1ft 9in gauge railway, opened in 1933, can be enjoyed. Motive power includes three diesel-powered steam outline locos supplied by Hudswell Clarke in 1933-35, including one based on the LMS 'Princess Royal' class. The site has been much-developed down the years and attracts some five million visitors each year. (Chris Spring)

62.   The station affords plenty of cover for returning revellers. 'Pacer' no. 142038 runs in from Preston on 8th October 2018. A Blackpool Pleasure Beach leaflet from the same year is shown on the opposite page. (Tom Heavyside)

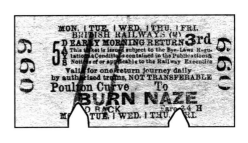

WEST OF KIRKHAM & WESHAM

63.   Soon after passing Kirkham North Junction, on the 6¾ miles long direct line to Blackpool between Bradkirk and Plumpton signal boxes, class 5 4-6-0 no. 44940 hurries towards its destination with an excursion from Colne on Sunday 7th June 1964. Behind the train are the tracks leading to Blackpool North and Fleetwood, with Weeton signal box 600 yards or so to the left (see picture 78). Officially closed as a through route in February 1967, about one mile of the down line from Kirkham North Junction was later utilised for dumping spent ballast from permanent-way renewals. A second siding/loop was laid in 1988. The last such trains were reported in the mid-1990s, but some of the rails remain in situ, albeit somewhat overgrown. Meanwhile further west the former trackbed became submerged under the M55 Motorway: opened from the M6 at Preston in 1975, it provides a convenient road into the heart of Blackpool (see picture 66). (Chris Spring)

BLACKPOOL SOUTH

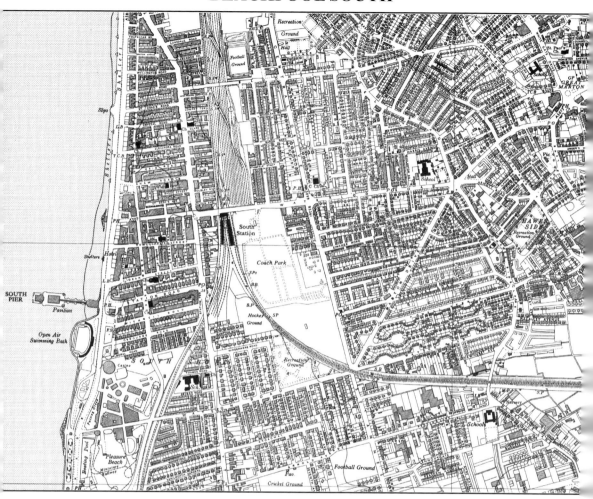

XVI.   This 1955 extract shows the two routes from Kirkham merging at the station, the Marton line on the right by a large coach park. Known as Waterloo Road when opened on completion of the direct line in May 1903, the station also served the coastal route from 14th July 1916 when South Shore Lytham Road station, 300 yards to the south, was abandoned. The name was amended to Blackpool South on 17th March 1932. Beyond Waterloo Road bridge were a vast array of sidings which extended north towards Central station. During the 1950s and early 1960s, at weekends from Eastertide onwards until the incomparable Blackpool Illuminations were switched off at the beginning of November, the sidings were regularly chock-full of excursion stock, with on occasions empty carriages having to be taken down the line, even as far as Kirkham, for stabling pending the time to return home.

64. Observed from the platform frequented by trains following the coastal route inland via St Annes, Saltley (Birmingham)-based 'Crab' no. 42790 comes off the Marton line with an extra from Burnley, en route to Blackpool Central on 19th July 1961. A poster for Kodak colour film – a favourite medium for many railway cameramen in the past – is among many advertisements taking up wall space. Except for one month spent at Kettering in June 1963, the Mogul was shedded at Saltley from July 1945 until its withdrawal in July 1963. (Frank Dean/E.M.Johnson coll.)

65. 'Black 5' 4-6-0 no. 45351 is about to travel inland via the Marton line on its way to Darwen on 17th May 1964. The 9K shed plate identifies it as belonging to Bolton shed. The width of the island platform, nos 3 and 4, is apparent. The canopies to the left protected platforms 1 and 2 that served the route via St Annes. On the right Eastern Region coaching stock is stabled on the up passenger loop. While the Marton line was abandoned as a through route in February 1967, a two-mile length east of here was retained until 1971 to serve Marton Gas Works. (Chris Spring)

66.   For a few years the station assumed more importance when the route beyond to Blackpool Central was closed to passengers in November 1964, that is until May 1970 when the main services serving the town were diverted to Blackpool North. Later, when the line from St Annes was reduced to one track in March 1982, only platform 1 remained available to passengers. The removal of the platform canopies allowed an unrestricted view of the substantial station building on Waterloo Road, that straddled the former lines to Central station. However, the demolition men were soon to move in and while the bridge remains, it is only road vehicles that now pass beneath at the end of Yeadon Way, an extension from the M55 Motorway. A class 108 diesel unit awaits departure time with the 09.20 to Kirkham on 3rd July 1984. (Noel Machell)

67.   Passengers who have arrived at their destination aboard 'Pacer' no. 142038, the 11.36 service from Preston, walk towards the exit on 18th October 2018. Within a couple of minutes the driver and guard had swapped ends and the unit was on its way back inland at 12.16. As regards the station, with the bare minimum of facilities (although there is plenty of car parking spaces available on the vacated land to the left), it can hardly be described as a fitting gateway to one of Britain's premier tourist resorts! The 'Pacer' has since moved to the heritage Mid-Norfolk Railway based at Dereham, where it arrived in February 2020. (Tom Heavyside)

NORTH OF BLACKPOOL SOUTH
Blackpool Engine Shed

68. The eight-road Blackpool Central shed received a new steel-framed roof in 1957-58. The allocation also covered the duties of its sub-shed serving North station (see pictures 110 and 111), just 1¼ miles away but 16 miles by rail via Kirkham North Junction. The depot was coded 24E by the LMS in 1935, this being retained apart from a short spell as 28A in 1950-52, until September 1963. Its last months were spent as 10B. In January 1960 the shed foreman had a total of 42 steam locomotives at his disposal, including 40 to former LMS designs consisting of eight class 3 2-6-2Ts, six class 4 2-6-4Ts, 20 class 5 4-6-0s, and six 'Jubilee' class 4-6-0s, plus two BR Standard class 4 2-6-4Ts. Here from the left 'Black 5' 4-6-0s nos 45404 visiting from Willesden shed (London) and 45495 from Warrington Dallam, keep company with home-based 'Jubilee' 4-6-0 no. 45705 *Seahorse* and class 4 2-6-4T no. 80093 on 6th March 1960. Behind no. 45495 is a class 3 2-6-2T while other locos shelter under cover. The 2-6-2Ts had been a familiar sight at the head of local services on the Fylde since 1954, but by July 1962 all had either left for pastures new or been withdrawn. (P.Reeves/Manchester Locomotive Society coll.)

69. The changing face of visiting motive power in late summer 1964, as a member of the old order, 'Black 5' no. 45205 from Rose Grove (Burnley), keeps company with a couple of diesels, an English Electric Type 4 1Co-Co1 and a Brush Type 2 A1A-A1A. The latter pair had arrived earlier with excursions from the east side of the Pennines. The coaling stage can be seen on the left along with the large water tank. The facilities were stretched to the limit on summer weekends, some locomotives having to be stabled in adjacent sidings pending their return home. Even at this late stage in the depot's life (it closed 2nd November 1964) a neat and tidy appearance was maintained.
(Peter Ward/RCTS coll.)

↓ 70. The imposing entrance to the station as taxis queue for business under the wide portico. Passengers whose trains departed from the excursion platforms 7 to 14 were directed to the entrance to the left on Central Drive. Tickets to London could then be purchased for 55s (£2-75). (David Lawrence/Photos from the Fifties)

← XVII. Originally plain Blackpool when opened by the Blackpool & Lytham Railway in 1863, it was renamed Blackpool Hounds Hill in 1872, before the suffix Central was adopted in June 1878. The survey indicates the convenience of the main station entrance to the Promenade, the 'Golden Mile' and other attractions, along with the uncovered excursion platforms located off Central Drive. Overnight accommodation could be had at myriad establishments in the surrounding streets. Outside the station on Saturdays young lads, some with home-made handcarts, would tout for business among the throngs of expectant incomers, ready to assist with baggage to their lodgings for a few pence. At the bottom edge, south of the gas works, is a section of the engine shed and attendant turntable. Between South and Central stations there was no less than 22 miles of track. Central Pier jutting out into the Irish Sea, by the Lifeboat Station, is one of three at the resort, the others North and South. On the seaward side of the main highway, by the Promenade is the tramway which continues north along the coast to Fleetwood.

71.   During Barton Wright's tenure as Chief Locomotive Superintendent of the Lancashire & Yorkshire Railway, the company took delivery between 1877 and 1879 of 32 0-4-4Ts. Kitson's built 12 while Dübs and Neilson supplied 10 each. A further 40 were received from Sharp Stewart during 1885-86. The last was withdrawn in 1913 but a number, with their rear driving wheels and motion removed, were retained as stationary boilers for carriage warming purposes. Two such survivors standing bunker to bunker between the main station platforms on the left and the open-air excursion platforms, understood to be L&YR nos 480 and 910 of Sharp Stewart origin and taken out of service in 1910, were recorded over 50 years later on 27th May 1962. Conspicuous are the 20ft extensions to the chimneys, which needed guide cables to ensure stability. Opened in May 1894, the iconic 518ft tall Blackpool Tower presides over the scene.
(John Marshall/Kidderminster Railway Museum coll.)

72.   As the end of the station's life drew near, locally-allocated 2-6-4T no. 42657 was station pilot on 2nd September 1964. At the adjacent platform 4-6-0 no. 45336 awaits departure time with the 6.30pm to Manchester Victoria. The latter was shedded at Newton Heath (Manchester) from October 1950 until withdrawn in January 1967. The side tank was transferred to Barrow later that September, only to be condemned two months later. (A.C.Gilbert/Manchester Locomotive Society coll.)

73. In late summer 1964, as some of the last passengers mill around the concourse, the statutory notice of 'Withdrawal of Railway Passenger Services' on 2nd November 1964 is prominently displayed. Maybe the two ladies walking towards the camera were on their way to see Decca recording stars The Bachelors at one of the resort's many theatres, seats costing 7s (35p) in the centre stalls and 5s (25p) in the side stalls. Among other adverts high above, Victory V gum lozenges were recommended for cold journeys! Little doubt staff in the left luggage office on the right, particularly at weekends, were kept very busy, likewise the newsagents. Sadly, from November the large roller blind detailing train departure times, destinations and from which platform, would become defunct. This was all to be swept away, but subsequent grandiose plans for a super-casino on the site never materalised, while a more modest amusement complex together with a multi-storey car park were relatively short-lived. (Manchester Locomotive Society coll.)

74. Since the late 1960s an inestimable number of cars have been parked along the old trackbed from Blackpool South. This was the scene from a standpoint close by that of picture 72 on the evening of 10th August 2019. (Tom Heavyside)

2. Kirkham & Wesham to Fleetwood
WEST OF KIRKHAM & WESHAM

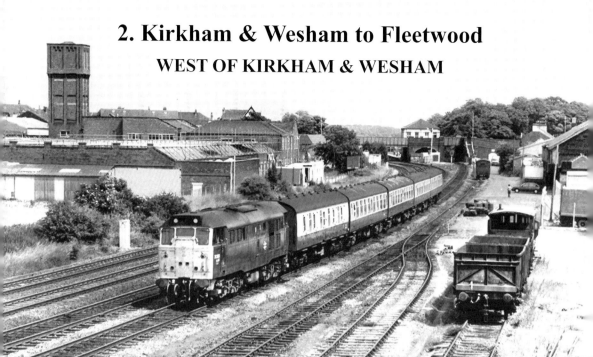

75. Having called at Kirkham & Wesham, to be seen in the background, no. 31280 proceeds along the down slow line towards Kirkham North Junction (see pictures 31 to 35) with the 13.50 from Manchester Victoria to Blackpool North on 18th June 1988. A few wagons and a brakevan occupy the goods sidings. The former Phoenix mill chimney which overlooked the area, had been felled. This class 31, which began life as no. D5810 in August 1961, was nearing the end of its active life, being declared surplus to requirements four months later in October 1988. (Tom Heavyside)

76. Viewed from a similar vantage point as the previous picture, the first AC electric locomotive to venture to Blackpool, privately-owned no. E3137 *Les Ross* powers an excursion from London Euston towards the junction on 13th April 2019. The wisp of steam at the rear of the train is emanating from 'Jubilee' class 4-6-0 no. 5690 *Leander*, which had been attached at Preston ready for the next stage of the special's itinerary. The new track layout completed during the electrification work can be studied, as can the rebuilding and extensions carried out by Fox's buscuits (relished by many since 1853) to their premises since the previous picture was taken. No. E3137 was released new from BR's Doncaster Works in January 1966, later being renumbered 86045 then 86259. Prior to retirement in October 2003, before preservation beckoned, it regularly passed through Preston on main line duties. (Tom Heavyside)

77. 'Crab' no. 42832 approaches Kirkham North Junction from the west with chemical tanks from Burn Naze on 12th September 1964. It is signalled onto the up fast line through Kirkham station. The rails in the foreground led to Blackpool Central via the Marton line, while behind the train, descending from the flyover above the Poulton lines on the extreme left, is the up passenger loop from the Marton route. No. 42832 was one of 70 of the class assembled at Horwich Works, the other 175 being put together at Crewe. The loco was deleted from capital stock in March 1965. (Chris Spring)

78. The small signal box at Weeton (it only had 10 levers), an intermediate block post between Bradkirk and Singleton, was perched on top of the cutting, close by the B5260 road overbridge. Its elevated position allowed the 'bobby' an uninterrupted view of approaching trains from either direction, although in later years it was often switched out. Here one of the ubiquitous class 47s no. 47426 (a total of 512 were built between 1962 and 1967) rushes by the unmanned box with the five-coach 17.10 Blackpool North to Crewe service on 19th July 1980. The M55 Motorway bridges the line just beyond the rear coach. Nearer the eye, the signal box looks in desperate need of a paintbrush! (Tom Heavyside)

79.   Under the supervision of the 44-lever Poulton No. 1 signal box, just to the left of the author, class 8F 2-8-0 no. 48730 slowly reverses away from a mixed freight, which it had hauled from the Fleetwood direction on 6th May 1968. The loco then travelled back through Poulton station, visible behind the wagons, as is the 50-lever Poulton No. 2 signal box, in order to turn on the triangle of lines beyond the station (see map XVIII), before returning to its train and continuing towards Preston. The tracks in the foreground led to Poulton goods yard, which was the original path to Fleetwood and Blackpool before the other lines in view were opened in 1896. No. 48730 was based at Rose Grove shed (Burnley) and survived until the very end of regular steam on BR in August 1968. (Tom Heavyside)

Poulton Goods

80.   After the new improved layout was opened at Poulton in 1896, the former passenger station survived as a goods depot until the end of 1968. It was photographed looking towards Kirkham on 12th April 1964. The level crossing gates on Breck Road remained, as did the rails set in the road. (John Marshall/Kidderminster Railway Museum coll.)

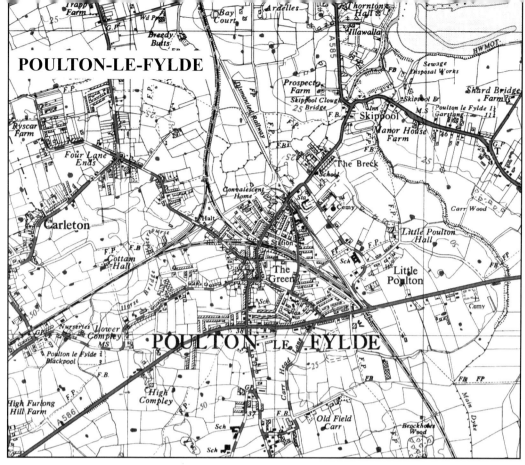

POULTON-LE-FYLDE

XVIII. This details the layout from 1896, the new station being much more convenient to the town centre than the original, and includes the triangle of lines created west of the station. Poulton Goods is marked 'Sta' on the map and the branch junction is above the letter 'D' of 'FYLDE'.

81. Looking towards the coast from midway along the island platform on 21st July 1962, we can count just some of the semaphore signals that controlled the complex of lines. To the left of no. 42294, a class 4 2-6-4T, standing light engine in the carriage siding, are the up and down fast lines. Meanwhile 'Jubilee' 4-6-0 no. 45661 *Vernon* has permission to leave with the 10.40am from Blackpool North to Manchester Victoria. Bottom right are the points in respect of the crossovers between the occupied up slow and loop lines. These were in regular use in steam days, when trains that had started from Blackpool or Fleetwood were joined together here before continuing their journey east. (Manchester Locomotive Society coll.)

82. A few passengers make their way towards the exit, after alighting from a class 47-hauled eleven-coach train bound for Blackpool North, as class 25 no. 25151 returns from the coast with the empty stock of an earlier arrival on 2nd July 1973. In the intervening years since the previous picture the layout had been rationalised, and apart from the platform roads only the carriage siding remained. Of the five signal boxes that originally controlled the area only Poulton No. 3 was then needed (see picture 85). The gas lamps along the platform in 1962 have given way to electricity – no need for a porter to walk the length turning them on and off. (Tom Heavyside)

← 83. During the late 1990s a refurbishment programme was completed, including restoration of the large clocks and reglazing the canopies. Hanging baskets and other floral displays enhance the scene at this award-winning station. At 14.38 on 17th September 2014 'Sprinter' no. 150207 slows to a halt after travelling across the Pennines from Huddersfield via Manchester.
(Tom Heavyside)

84. In 2018 the canopies were cut-back slightly to provide sufficient clearance for overhead electrified wires. Completion has allowed class 390 'Pendolinos', previously confined to the West Coast main line, to serve Blackpool, although they do not stop here: on 31st July 2018 a Virgin Trains nine-vehicle formation passes with the 10.36 from London Euston. Even so the 20,000 plus inhabitants of this pleasant market town (an increase from 12,726 in 1961), have a choice of four trains most hours towards either Blackpool or Preston. Today a small plaque by the entrance on Breck Road, seen above, outlines the station's history, highlighting the fact it was once an important junction for holiday excursion traffic with its platform 348m long, and that the station also catered for boat train passengers sailing from Fleetwood. (Tom Heavyside)

Railway Station

This station, opened in 1896 was owned by the Lancashire & Yorkshire and LNWR joint companies and replaced the original Preston & Wyre Railway station at the corner of Station Road and the Breck which was opened in 1840. An important junction for holiday excursion traffic with its platforms 348 metres long, this station also catered for boat train passengers sailing from Fleetwood.

NORTH OF POULTON-LE-FYLDE

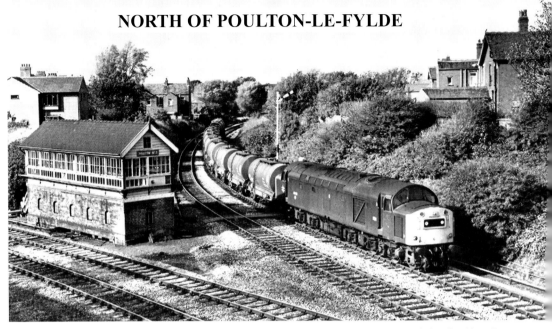

85.   Class 40 no. 40158 has permission from Poulton No. 3 signal box to join the line from Blackpool North, and proceed through Poulton station with a set of caustic soda tanks from ICI Burn Naze on 14th October 1983. The box with 74 levers was the largest of the five boxes at Poulton, and the only one in use after December 1977 when No. 1 box closed. (Tom Heavyside)

86.   A class 37 rounds the curve from Poulton station and passes the former junction with the line from Blackpool, in charge of an oil train for Burn Naze during the summer of 1993. The demolished Poulton No. 5 signal box, which controlled the junction, stood below right, while the trackbed of the spur to Poulton No. 4 box is clearly visible. Both boxes closed on 18th July 1971. From December 1973 trains in both directions used the former down line, although the up line remained in situ. The tower of St Chad's church in the centre of Poulton rises above the treetops on the left. (Russell Moorhouse)

THORNTON-CLEVELEYS

XIX.   Trains halted here for a brief period in 1842-43 when it was known as Ramper (Road). Reopened as Cleveleys in April 1865 on the south side of the road, it was renamed Thornton for Cleveleys in April 1905. The current platforms were laid on the north side of the highway in 1925: it became Thornton-Cleveleys in February 1953. The coast at Cleveleys lies some two miles west of the station. The goods yard features on the west side of the railway, between the station and Hillylaid crossing. This 6ins to 1 mile map is dated 1955.

↓ 87. Members of the 30-strong BR Standard class 2 2-6-2Ts were regularly to be seen along the Fleetwood branch from June 1954, when nos 84016-19 were transferred from Bury to Fleetwood shed, with others following in later years. The first 20 were built at Crewe Works in 1953, with the remaining 10 appearing from Darlington in 1957. Here no. 84018 clatters over the level crossing en route to Fleetwood on 10th August 1964. The loco had collected the two coaches at Poulton, where they had been detached from a train emanating from Manchester Victoria, the main portion continuing to Blackpool North. The man in charge of the signal box operated a 22-lever frame. The end of the platform canopy can be glimpsed top right. The station closed six years later on 1st June 1970. On occasions the Candy Box opposite the station could well have been a distraction for young trainspotters. (Chris Spring)

→ 88. With only the former down line still in use, no. 40158 passes the same spot with some incoming tanks for ICI at Burn Naze on 14th October 1983. Note the cover over the redundant train describer panel is of a different design to that at the other end of the loco (see picture 85). The shop opposite now traded as Victoria Wine Stores. When the line was singled in December 1973, the signal box was downgraded to gate box status, that is until 15th November 1987 when it became the responsibility of men travelling on the trains to ensure their safe passage over the road, along with that at Hilly Laid (spelt as two words on railway documentation) crossing a little further north. (Tom Heavyside)

↓ 89. The Poulton & Wyre Railway Society was founded in 2006 with the ambition of reopening the railway between Poulton and Fleetwood. Under their stewardship the station has been completely refurbished, and looks quite resplendent as seen on 13th April 2019, although sadly the signal box has been demolished and the level crossing gates replaced by a picket fence. The small semaphore and disc signals stand where the previous semaphore signals stood, but face the opposite direction. The track stretches towards Fleetwood, but there is no trace of the former goods yard (closed March 1969), which was just beyond the end of the down platform on the left. Trains are still awaited, although some encouraging news was received in July 2022, when following an earlier business case submission by local stakeholders, the Department of Transport announced the Poulton to Fleetwood route was among nine schemes to be granted further development funding under the Government's Restoring Your Railway programme. In recent times suggestions have also been made that the Blackpool tramway should be extended from Fleetwood to Poulton utilising the former rail route. (Tom Heavyside)

NORTH OF THORNTON-CLEVELEYS

ICI Hillhouse Works

90. A John Fowler 0-4-0 diesel-mechanical loco is driven out of the brick-built two-road shed on 18th August 1981. The loco was built in 1952, maker's no. 4210058. A visitor to the cab seems to be enjoying the occasion. (C.Shepherd/ copyright Industrial Railway Society)

91. The sprawling Hillhouse site is surveyed from the cab of class 40 no. 40028, named *Samaria* (a former Cunard ocean liner) in its early days as no. D228, as it enters the reception sidings during the summer of 1984. A Rolls Royce four-wheeled diesel-hydraulic loco, built in 1965 at their Sentinel Works, Shrewsbury, waits to shunt the incoming wagons. In the middle distance on the left is Burn Naze South signal box, which remained in use until August 1987, the chimney beyond is part of ICI's power station complex. (Russell Moorhouse)

BURN NAZE

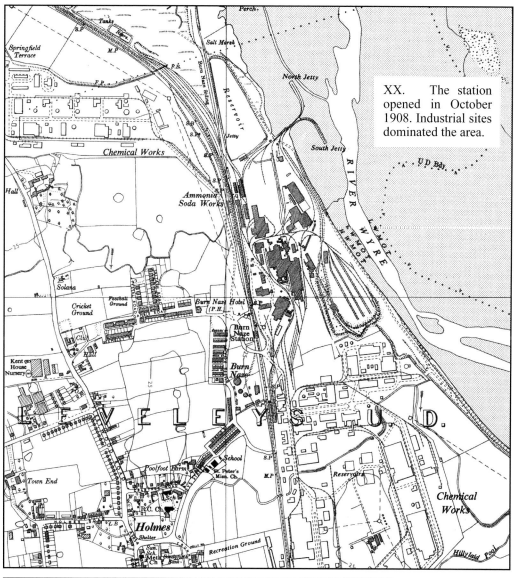

XX. The station opened in October 1908. Industrial sites dominated the area.

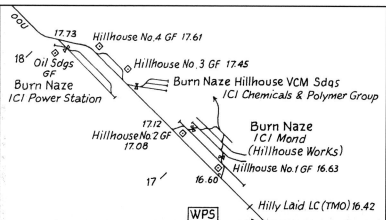

XXI. The diagram details the branch status in 1990. The line beyond the ICI Power Station was by this time out of use. Freight traffic to the ICI Hillhouse Works continued until 1999. (©TRACKmaps)

92. A two-car DMU manufactured by the Cravens Railway Carriage & Wagon Company at their Sheffield factory in 1957, nos M50778 and M50811 (later designated class 105), pause while en route from Blackpool North to Fleetwood on 10th August 1964. A family watch proceedings from road level. This was the last summer of the direct service between the two towns. (Chris Spring)

NORTH OF BURN NAZE

93. A 'Black 5' in pieces. During July 1981 no. 45491 was transported from Woodham's scrapyard at Barry, South Wales, to ICI's Thornton Power Station, on the west side of the main line, where work soon started on its restoration. Six years later the components were transferred to the nearby Fleetwood Locomotive Centre (see next two pictures); the engine is now based on the Great Central Railway at Loughborough. (Russell Moorhouse)

Fleetwood Locomotive Centre

94.   The former coal-fired Fleetwood Power Station generated electricity from 1955 until its closure in 1981. After the vast majority of the buildings had been cleared, a preservation centre was established on the site during the mid-1980s. Shortly after its arrival in 1987, *Margaret*, a Hudswell Clarke 0-4-0 diesel-mechanical loco, supplied new in 1956 to the British Petroleum Isle of Grain Refinery in Kent with a National 128hp engine, receives attention outside the shed. The chimney (see picture 19) had been removed. A vintage tractor completes the scene. *Margaret* now resides at the Ribble Steam Railway at Preston. (Russell Moorhouse)

95.   *The King*, an 0-4-0 well tank constructed by E.Borrows & Sons of St Helens for the local glass industry in 1906, gingerly picks its way along the overgrown sidings with a four-plank wagon and a van in tow on 2nd September 1997. This was the last running day at the centre before closure. At present *The King* is at The Flour Mill at Bream in the Forest of Dean, Gloucestershire. (Tom Heavyside)

Fleetwood Engine Shed

96. The six-road depot was conveniently located near the dock area. In January 1960 when coded 24F, it had an allocation of 27 steam locos, including seven class 2 2-6-2Ts (three of LMS origin and four to BR Standard specifications), 10 'Crab' 2-6-0s and five 'Black 5' 4-6-0s. For shunting the dock sidings the shed maintained two short wheel-based 0-6-0Ts built at Derby by the LMS in 1928, and three veteran ex-L&YR 0-6-0STs from the Victorian era, the eldest no. 51336 then 82 years of age. In April 1965 during the shed's last full year of operation, 25 steam locos were listed on the depot's register, 23 with a LMS pedigree - two class 4 2-6-4Ts, 11 'Black 5' 4-6-0s, two 'Jinty' 0-6-0Ts and eight class 8F 2-8-0s - along with two BR Standard class 2 2-6-2Ts. Dock shunting was then the preserve of three of the short-lived class 02 170hp 0-4-0 diesel-hydraulic locos, which made their debut new from the Yorkshire Engine Company in September/October 1961. The last of the trio to be withdrawn, no. D2860 in December 1970, can now be seen at the National Railway Museum at York. From September 1963, following a reorganisation of motive power districts, the engines sported 10C shed plates. Outside the shed in 1963, two 'Black 5' 4-6-0s, two Standard class 2 2-6-2Ts and a 'Crab' 2-6-0, await their next assignments. (Peter Ward/RCTS coll.)

➔ 97. Home-based 8F 2-8-0 no. 48223 has its tender replenished in the enclosed 'coal hole' on 1st October 1964. Coal was shovelled from 16 ton wagons shunted to the higher level. Wyre Dock Junction signal box is in view on the right. The 8F was among eight redeployed to the Fylde from the East Midlands in November 1963, their influx effectively bringing to an end the shed's long association with the 'Crabs', which were all moved away the following summer. On the shed's demise, on 14th February 1966, no. 48223 was transferred to Rose Grove (Burnley), where it had previously spent three months from June 1965, before returning to Fleetwood. The site was subsequently used as a coal concentration depot until 1983. (RCTS coll)

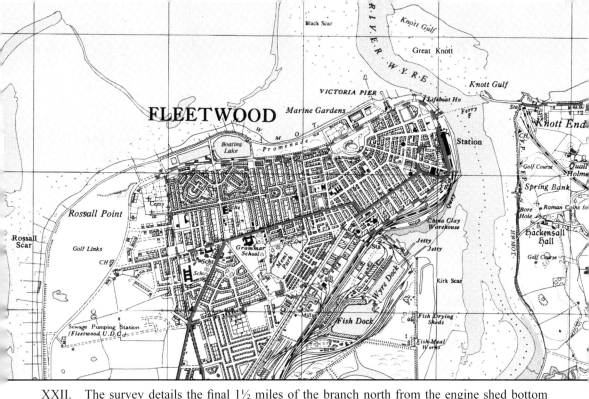

XXII.   The survey details the final 1½ miles of the branch north from the engine shed bottom centre. Wyre Dock station, opened 1st December 1885, is by the northern corner of the dock area, with the terminal Fleetwood station near the mouth of the River Wyre. The 10-acre Wyre Dock and a five-acre timber pond were engineered by the L&YR and in use from October 1877. The latter was enlarged to 15 acres between 1906 and 1908 to cater for the expanding fish trade. In fact Fleetwood was once one of Britain's busiest fishing ports, in 1961 a considerable proportion of the town's 29,000 or so inhabitants relying on the sea for their well-being, with much of the catch being despatched by rail until the late 1960s. Extensive sidings served the dock complex. The historic tramway from Blackpool is identified along the road that runs parallel to the railway from by the engine shed, although the last three-quarter mile of the tramway, to a loop near Fleetwood station has been omitted.

Fleetwood Docks

98.   Octogenarian class 2F no. 51419 takes a breather while on Target (trip as required goods engine turn) no. 39 during its last days on active service. The loco was manufactured by Kitson for the L&YR as an 0-6-0 tender engine in May 1880, but rebuilt as an 0-6-0 saddle tank at Horwich Works in October 1895. It was withdrawn in September 1961. In the background, overlooked on the right by the cooling towers of Fleetwood Power Station, many vans await the next haul of fish. Nowadays very little fish is landed at Fleetwood, mainly pleasure craft being moored in the docks, while the area depicted here serves as a retail park. Happily the renowned extra strong Fisherman's Friend lozenges, developed in Fleetwood back in 1865 to help fishermen combat the severe weather conditions encountered in Icelandic waters, are still produced in the town, and now in a variety of flavours. (P.Reeves/Manchester Locomotive Society coll.)

WYRE DOCK

99. A two-car DMU consisting of nos M51942 and M52057, built at Derby Works in January 1961 and later designated class 108, is about to stop at the island platform with the 3.45pm departure from Fleetwood to Blackpool North on 11th May 1963. Note the small yellow warning panel on the front of the leading vehicle. Access to the station was by way of the footbridge, which linked Dock Street on the left and the dock area. (Chris Spring)

100. BR Standard class 2 2-6-2T no. 84010 (a Fleetwood-based engine since December 1959) has permission to leave for the remaining half-mile of its journey to Fleetwood on 19th May 1964. A supply of gas was relied on for lighting. A connection to the extensive docks sidings is visible in the left foreground. (John Marshall/Kidderminster Railway Museum coll.)

101.   While looking in the opposite direction on 10th August 1964, members of the permanent-way gang stand aside, as sister 2-6-2T no. 84018 draws two coaches forming the 11.25am from Fleetwood to Poulton over the level crossing. The gates were swung back and forth across the road by means of a large wheel inside the 40-lever signal box depicted in picture 99. Popular cars of the period, a Ford Anglia and a Morris Minor, are stationary on Dock Street. The line was truncated here on 18th April 1966, when this became the branch terminus, the footbridge being removed and a level access created from the roadway, along with a new booking hall and waiting area. The station signage and timetables were amended to read 'Fleetwood' from the same date. In turn the station was closed on 1st June 1970. (Chris Spring)

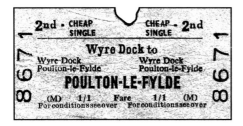

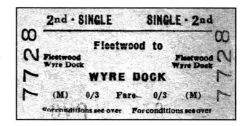

FLEETWOOD

102.   The station welcomed its first passengers on 15th July 1883, when a half-mile extension beyond the previous terminus was opened, the new facility being adjacent to a railway-owned landing-stage, brought into use 10 weeks earlier. In past times the platforms were often thronged with passengers transferring to and from the steamers that served destinations across the Irish Sea. This persisted post World War II, particularly on summer Saturdays, when thousands of holiday-makers arrived by train on their way to Douglas on the Isle of Man (the Belfast sailings ended in 1928). However, by January 1961 the BR-owned landing-stage was becoming unsafe and deemed unecomic to repair. Thus, sadly, later that year, the last regular Isle of Man ferry set sail from Fleetwood on 11th September. From then on the station became much quieter, as here on 19th May 1964, when with the Wyre estuary on the right, another of the Fleetwood-allocated 2-6-2Ts no. 84016 bides time at platform 3, ready to leave with four coaches. The buffer-stops for platforms 2 and 3 were positioned just outside the 82ft-wide station roof, while platforms 1 (left) and 4 extended much further back towards the ticket barriers. A fifth platform was available outside the post and wire fence on the right. Electricity had replaced gas for lighting purposes in the late 1950s. Closed on 18th April 1966, walking by the river today there is no clue that the station or ferry berths ever existed. (John Marshall/Kidderminster Railway Museum coll.)

North Euston Hotel

103a. The elegant Greek classical style semicircular frontage and portico of the 1841-completed hotel, overlooks the Wyre estuary. Recorded on 12th September 2018, it stands as a permanent reminder of Fleetwood's past railway importance, in its early days travellers bedding here for the night prior to boarding a ferry to Ireland, Scotland or elsewhere. To the left of the author, across from the hotel in Euston Park, looking out to sea and unveiled in May 2018, is a life-size statue in bronze of Sir Peter Hesketh-Fleetwood, 1801-66, founder of the town. A short walk away is the landing-stage for the Knott End ferry, which has been plying the Wyre since 1894, crossing at half-hour intervals when the tide permits. The terminus for the standard gauge tramway from Blackpool is also near the hotel - the journey between the two towns is detailed in our *Blackpool Tramways 1933-66* and *Triumphant Tramways of England* albums. (Tom Heavyside)

103b. The *Wyre Rose* providing the ferry service to Knott End, anchored at Fleetwood on 4th April 2023. Knott End is in view across the water.
(Tom Heavyside)

3. Poulton-le-Fylde to Blackpool North

SOUTH OF POULTON-LE-FYLDE

104. Class 50 no. 50040 rumbles by Poulton No. 3 signal box and the junction with the Fleetwood line, as it prepares to halt with the 18.20 service from Blackpool North to London Euston, on the rather dull evening of 12th July 1975. No. 50040 hauled the train as far as Preston where it was relieved by an electric loco. Rodding and wires connected to the signal box can be seen either side of the picture. Clear indentations in the ballast near the retaining wall on the left indicate the position of the former fast lines. No. 50040 was among 50 of the class initially leased by BR from English Electric, after completion at their Newton-le-Willows, Lancashire factory between October 1967 and December 1968. At first numbered D400 to D449, they were fitted with a 2,700hp engine, had a Co-Co wheel arrangement and a top speed of 100mph. Later purchased by BR, no. 50040 was one of 12 retained by the LMR in May 1974, following electrification of the West Coast main line north from Preston. It joined the rest of the class on the Western Region in April 1976, where it was named *Leviathan* in September 1978. It remained on the books of BR until August 1990. (Tom Heavyside)

105. Seen from the same vantage point, electric unit no. 319363 glides by with the 13.05 from Blackpool North to Liverpool Lime Street on 31st July 2018. The need for the former signal box had been eliminated and the lines towards Fleetwood severed. The tracks in the Blackpool direction had been realigned and a 70mph speed restriction sign erected by the telecommunications mast. Note the signal post by the former up line from Fleetwood still stands, although latterly there had been no need to climb quite so high as previously to attend to the lamp! Poulton Congregational Church top left still stands but now converted to apartments, the congregation as part of the United Reformed Church, utilising a more modern building nearby. (Tom Heavyside)

106. Looking back from Tithebarn Street overbridge (seen in the previous two pictures), with the station frontage protruding above Breck Road, no. 47455 sets off from Poulton on the last leg of its journey to Blackpool with an extra from Edinburgh on 2nd July 1983. This class 47 was released new from Crewe Works in April 1964 as no. D1575, being renumbered 47455 in February 1974. It was withdrawn in March 1990. (Tom Heavyside)

107. Turning to look towards Blackpool on the same day, the driver of a Swindon class 120 cross-country unit has authority to proceed from Poulton No 3 signal box with a train destined for Manchester Victoria. The six-car formation has just passed the site of Poulton No. 4 signal box (closed July 1971), which controlled the former junction with the Fleetwood line. The trackbed of the latter can be glimpsed above the rear carriages. The distant signal by the down line, indicates the gates at Carleton level crossing have yet to be opened for an approaching train on its way to Blackpool. (Tom Heavyside)

LAYTON

XXIII. Known as Bispham from its opening in May 1867 until July 1938, when it became Layton (Lancs). The suffix has been dropped in recent times. It serves a mainly residential area.

108. Staff were withdrawn in May 1994. The former station master's house is now privately owned. Here class 158 no. 158817 speeds by on the last stage of its journey from York to Blackpool on 17th September 2014. In preparation for electrification a new slightly higher footbridge had already been installed. The bridge seen in the background supporting the A587 Blackpool ring road was rebuilt later. (Tom Heavyside)

109. With the wires energised, passengers prepare to board no. 319374 forming the 09.27 Blackpool North to Hazel Grove service on 29th June 2019. We are able to study more closely the design of the footbridge, while the author remained under CCTV surveillance! (Tom Heavyside)

SOUTH OF LAYTON

Blackpool North Engine Shed

110. From 1935 the three-road brick-built shed was administered by the main Blackpool depot (see pictures 68 and 69), rather than having a separate allocation as previously. Alongside the south wall on 6th September 1962 is 'Jubilee' class 4-6-0 no. 45571 *South Africa*, built by the North British Locomotive Company at their Hyde Park works in Glasgow for the LMS in 1934. The loco had been based at Blackpool since June 1937, but spent its last days from November 1963 at Speke Junction shed (Liverpool), before its withdrawal the following May. The 'Black 5' nearer the photographer is unidentifiable. (K.Fairey/Colour-Rail.com)

111. The shed closed on 10th February 1964, and that summer any steam locomotives arriving at North station that required attention before their return, had to trek the 16 miles via Kirkham North Junction to Central shed. When the latter closed on 2nd November 1964 the shed was reactivated for servicing purposes and retained until the end of 1967. Here Type 4 diesel locomotives nos D305 (later no. 40105) and D1813 (later no. 47332), based at Willesden (London) and Saltley (Birmingham) respectively, intermingle with steam locos in the yard, after bringing trains into Blackpool on 19th June 1965. (Peter Ward/RCTS coll.)

BLACKPOOL NORTH

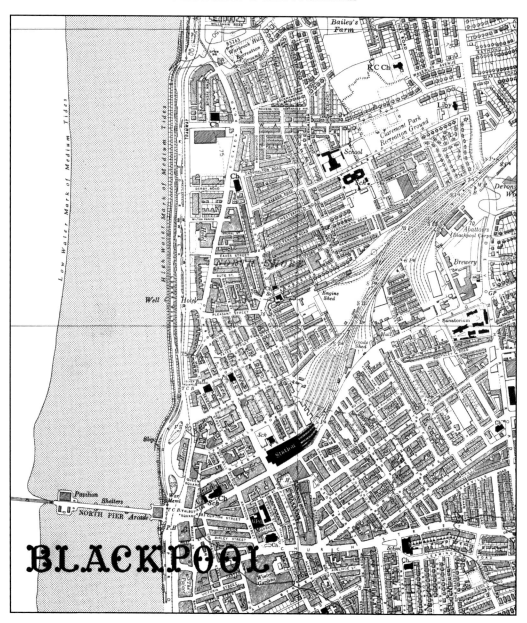

XXIV.   Originally plain Blackpool when opened in April 1846, Talbot Road was added in May 1872, before the suffix was amended to North in March 1932. The main platforms 1 to 6 (covered) are near the foot of this 1956 survey, with the unprotected excursion platforms 7 to 16 a little further inland. The engine shed and extensive carriage sidings are also recorded. As in the vicinity of Central station, accommodation was available in many of the surrounding streets. The attractions of the North Pier were but a short walk from the station down Talbot Road.

112.   A busy Dickson Road outside the station on 15th October 1960. A Blackpool Corporation tram has just terminated, and as a few passengers make their way towards the portico, the conductor prepares to transfer the trolley-wheel to the far end, before reattaching it to the overhead wire ready for its next journey to Fleetwood. The driver of a Ford Consul car is impeded by the process. The tramway service to the station ended on 27th October 1963. (Colour-Rail.com)

113.   Only one former L&YR 0-4-4T, identity unknown, was required here for carriage heating purposes (see picture 71). In this undated photograph we can examine some of the connecting pipe-work needed in conjunction with its duties. The chimney extension has been attached to the side of the boiler, the position assumed when locos were being transported to Horwich Works for maintenance. Note the barricaded cab entrance to protect the fireman from the prevailing winds off the Irish Sea. Also the six-plank wagon containing coal supplies and the mess van behind. The loco was removed in 1962. (R.Butterfield/Initial Photographics)

114. 'Black 5' 4-6-0 no. 45205 pulls away from the main part of the station, returning half-a-dozen empty vans to Manchester on 2nd September 1966. A 'Jubilee' class 4-6-0 stands at the southern most excursion platform, these always open to the elements. No. 3 signal box guards the main platforms; erected in 1896, from 1924 it housed an 88-lever frame. (M.H.Yarley/Colour-Rail.com)

115. The sun doesn't always shine in Blackpool, but unless directed down Upper Queen Street to the excursion platforms, passengers were well-protected from wind and storms by the arched overall roof and canopies. 'Black 5' no. 45424 waits at platform 2, as a DMU rests at platform 5 during September 1967. (Colour-Rail.com)

116. An evocative view looking inland from the end of platform 4 on 16th January 1970. Relics from the steam age in the shape of the parachute water tanks and attendant braziers remain. Type 2 no. D5204 (later no. 25054) stands near Blackpool Station signal box (known earlier as Blackpool North No. 3), which controlled the main part of the station until its closure on 7th January 1973. (H.B.Priestley/Robert Humm coll.)

117.   From January 1973 trains utilised the former nos 9 to 16 excursion platforms; nos 1 to 6 and associated buildings subsequently being cleared, and the vacated land released for redevelopment. Platforms 7 and 8 were also abandoned. Later, at a time when loco haulage was necessary due to a shortage of DMUs, no. 31448 rolls towards the buffer stops at platform 6 (the former no. 14) with the 17.20 from Manchester Victoria on 18th June 1988. The station and its approaches was to remain one of the last bastions of semaphore signals pending electrification in 2018. The 94-lever Blackpool North No. 2 signal box can be seen on the left. Prior to 1973 it was normally open only during the main visitor season, when the excursion platforms were needed to cope with the vast volume of extras. The extensive carriage sidings fan out beyond the box. The loco began life at Brush Traction, Loughborough, as Type 2 (later class 31) no. D5566 in November 1959. It was withdrawn in July 1995. (Tom Heavyside)

118.   With the tower looming overhead, the eight platforms appear deserted on the evening of 13th July 1993, as 'Executive' liveried no. 37419 awaits departure time at platform 4 with the 20.27 to Manchester Victoria. 'Sprinter' no. 150149 is at platform 7. Beyond the individual platform access doors is a large enclosed circulating area, completed in January 1974. No cover has ever been provided along the platforms. The loco emerged from English Electric's Vulcan Foundry at Newton-le-Willows, Lancashire as Type 3 (later class 37) no. D6991 in June 1965. It remains extant in the employ of Direct Rail Services. (Tom Heavyside)

XXV.   Layout of the station and its approach as of 1990. (©TRACKmaps)

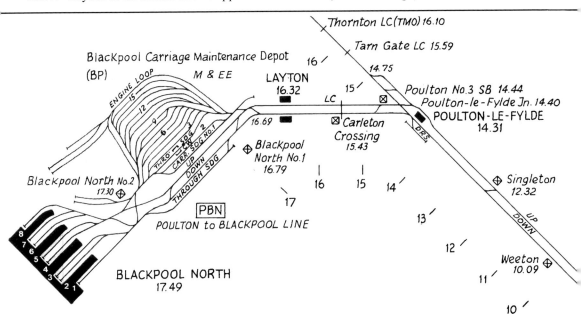

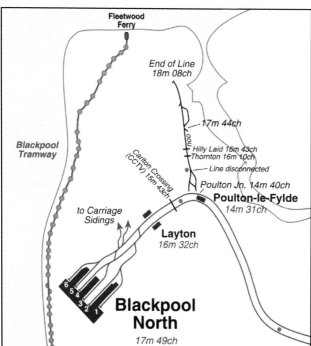

119. The station was closed for six months from November 2017, during which period the semaphore signals were disposed of, the rails realigned and three new island platforms constructed before the overhead wires were positioned. Following the reconstruction, ready to leave platform 5 at 11.27 bound for Hazel Grove is no. 319361 on 19th June 2019, while sister unit no. 319367 at platform 4 will start its next journey to Manchester Airport at 11.58. First to depart will be diesel-powered class 158 no. 158853 from platform 2 on the left, destined for York. (Tom Heavyside)

XXVI. The revamped layout (dated 2018) on completion of the electrification project.
(© TRACKmaps/
Platform 5 Publishing)

120.   Our excursion to the seaside ends outside today's unpretentious glass-fronted station. The 11-vehicle Virgin Trains class 390 'Pendolino' no. 390148 *Flying Scouseman*, just arrived from London Euston rests at platform 1, its passengers keeping the local taxi firms busy on 8th October 2018. The class 390s were completed by Alstom at their Washwood Heath factory, Birmingham, and made their debut in 2001. On sections of the West Coast main line south of Preston, no. 390148 would have been able to travel at up to 125mph, aided around curves by its tilting mechanism. Prior to 1973 the roadway in front of the station was occupied by the rails serving the former platforms 1 to 6 (see picture 116). A short section of the wall that formerly divided railway-owned land from Talbot Road is visible on the right-hand edge of the frame. This view was captured from the car park roof of a large retail store, which has since been demolished to make way for a much-delayed new tram terminus and hotel. The tracks have already been laid and thus shortly, after an interlude of 60 years, passengers bound for Fleetwood or south along the sea front, will once again be able to board a tram outside the station, albeit the approach is along Talbot Road from the North Pier, rather than Dickson Road as in earlier times (see picture 112). It will provide a welcome and fitting end to a journey across the Fylde.
(Tom Heavyside)

EVOLVING THE

Vic Mitchell and Keith Smith

ULTIMATE RAIL ENCYCLOPEDIA

INTERNATIONAL

126a Camelsdale Road, GU27 3RJ. Tel:01730 813169

A-978 0 906520 B- 978 1 873793 C- 978 1 901706 D-978 1 904474
E - 978 1 906008 F - 978 1 908174 G - 978 1 910356

Our RAILWAY titles are listed below. Please check availability by looking at our website **www.middletonpress.co.uk**, telephoning us or by requesting a Brochure which includes our LATEST RAILWAY TITLES also our TRAMWAY, TROLLEYBUS, MILITARY and COASTAL series.

email:info@middletonpress.co.uk

A
Abergavenny to Merthyr C 91 8
Abertillery & Ebbw Vale Lines D 84 5
Aberystwyth to Carmarthen E 90 1
Alnmouth to Berwick G 50 0
Alton - Branch Lines to A 11 6
Ambergate to Buxton G 28 9
Ambergate to Mansfield G 39 5
Andover to Southampton A 82 6
Ascot - Branch Lines around A 64 2
Ashburton - Branch Line to B 95 4
Ashford - Steam to Eurostar B 67 1
Ashford to Dover A 48 2
Austrian Narrow Gauge D 04 3
Avonmouth - BL around D 42 5
Aylesbury to Rugby D 91 3

B
Baker Street to Uxbridge D 90 6
Bala to Llandudno E 87 1
Banbury to Birmingham D 27 2
Banbury to Cheltenham E 63 5
Bangor to Holyhead F 01 7
Bangor to Portmadoc E 72 7
Barking to Southend C 80 2
Barmouth to Pwllheli E 53 6
Barry - Branch Lines around D 50 0
Bartlow - Branch Lines to F 27 7
Basingstoke to Salisbury A 89 4
Bath Green Park to Bristol C 36 9
Bath to Evercreech Junction A 60 4
Beamish 40 years on rails E94 9
Bedford to Wellingborough D 31 9
Berwick to Drem F 64 2
Berwick to St. Boswells F 75 8
B'ham to Tamworth & Nuneaton F 63 5
Birkenhead to West Kirby F 61 1
Birmingham to Wolverhampton E253
Blackburn to Hellifield F 95 6
Bletchley to Cambridge D 94 4
Bletchley to Rugby E 07 9
Bodmin - Branch Lines around B 83 1
Bolton to Preston G 61 6
Boston to Lincoln F 80 2
Bournemouth to Evercreech Jn A 46 8
Bradshaw's History F18 5
Bradshaw's Rail Times 1850 F 13 0
Branch Lines series - see town names
Brecon to Neath D 43 2
Brecon to Newport D 16 6
Brecon to Newtown E 06 2
Brighton to Eastbourne A 16 1
Brighton to Worthing A 03 1
Bristol to Taunton D 03 6
Bromley South to Rochester B 23 7
Bromsgrove to Birmingham D 87 6
Bromsgrove to Gloucester D 73 9
Broxbourne to Cambridge F16 1
Brunel - A railtour D 74 6
Bude - Branch Line to B 29 9
Burnham to Evercreech Jn B 68 0
Buxton to Stockport G 32 6

C
Cambridge to Ely D 55 5
Canterbury - BLs around B 58 9
Cardiff to Dowlais (Cae Harris) E 47 5
Cardiff to Pontypridd E 95 6
Cardiff to Swansea E 42 0
Carlisle to Beattock G 69 2
Carlisle to Hawick E 85 7
Carmarthen to Fishguard E 66 6
Caterham & Tattenham Corner B251
Central & Southern Spain NG E 91 8
Chard and Yeovil - BLs a C 30 7
Charing Cross to Orpington A 96 3
Cheddar - Branch Line to B 90 9
Cheltenham to Andover C 43 7
Cheltenham to Redditch D 81 4
Chesterfield to Lincoln G 21 0
Chester to Birkenhead F 21 5
Chester to Manchester F 51 2
Chester to Rhyl E 93 2
Chester to Warrington F 40 6
Chichester to Portsmouth A 14 7
Clacton and Walton - BLs to F 04 8
Clapham Jn to Beckenham Jn B 36 7
Cleobury Mortimer - BLs a E 18 5
Clevedon & Portishead - BLs to D180
Consett to South Shields E 57 4
Cornwall Narrow Gauge D 56 2
Corris and Vale of Rheidol E 65 9
Coventry to Leicester G 00 5
Craven Arms to Llandeilo E 35 2
Craven Arms to Wellington E 33 8
Crawley to Littlehampton A 34 5
Crewe to Manchester F 57 4
Crewe to Wigan G 12 8
Cromer - Branch Lines around C 26 0
Cromford and High Peak G 35 7
Croydon to East Grinstead B 48 0
Crystal Palace & Catford Loop B 87 1
Cyprus Narrow Gauge E 13 0

D
Darjeeling Revisited F 09 3
Darlington Leamside Newcastle E 28 4
Darlington to Newcastle D 98 2
Dartford to Sittingbourne B 34 3
Denbigh - Branch Lines around F 32 1
Derby to Chesterfield G 11 1
Derby to Nottingham G 45 6
Derby to Stoke-on-Trent F 93 2
Derwent Valley - BL to the D 06 7
Devon Narrow Gauge E 09 3
Didcot to Banbury D 02 9
Didcot to Swindon C 84 0
Didcot to Winchester C 13 0
Diss to Norwich G 22 7
Dorset & Somerset NG D 76 0
Douglas - Laxey - Ramsey E 75 8
Douglas to Peel C 88 8
Douglas to Port Erin C 55 0
Douglas to Ramsey D 39 5
Dover to Ramsgate A 78 9
Drem to Edinburgh G 06 7
Dublin Northwards in 1950s E 31 4
Dunstable - Branch Lines to E 27 7

E
Ealing to Slough C 42 0
Eastbourne to Hastings A 27 7
East Croydon to Three Bridges A 53 6
Eastern Spain Narrow Gauge E 56 7
East Grinstead - BLs to A 07 9
East Kent Light Railway A 61 1
East London - Branch Lines of C 44 4
East London Line B 80 0
East of Norwich - Branch Lines E 69 7
Effingham Junction - BLs a A 74 1
Ely to Norwich C 90 1
Enfield Town & Palace Gates D 32 6
Epsom to Horsham A 30 7
Eritrean Narrow Gauge E 38 3
Euston to Harrow & Wealdstone C 89 5
Exeter to Barnstaple B 15 2
Exeter to Newton Abbot C 49 9
Exeter to Tavistock B 69 5
Exmouth - Branch Lines to B 00 8

F
Fairford - Branch Line to A 52 9
Falmouth, Helston & St. Ives C 74 1
Fareham to Salisbury A 67 3
Faversham to Dover B 05 3
Felixstowe & Aldeburgh - BL to D 20 3
Fenchurch Street to Barking C 20 8
Festiniog - 50 yrs of enterprise C 83 3
Festiniog 1946-55 E 01 7
Festiniog in the Fifties B 68 8
Festiniog in the Sixties B 91 6
Ffestiniog in Colour 1955-82 F 25 3
Finsbury Park to Alexandra Pal C 02 8
French Metre Gauge Survivors F 88 8
Frome to Bristol B 77 0

G
Gainsborough to Sheffield G 17 3
Galashiels to Edinburgh F 52 9
Gloucester to Bristol D 35 7
Gloucester to Cardiff D 66 1
Gosport - Branch Lines around A 36 9
Greece Narrow Gauge D 72 2
Guildford to Redhill A 63 5

H
Hampshire Narrow Gauge D 36 4
Harrow to Watford D 14 2
Harwich & Hadleigh - BLs to F 02 4
Harz Revisited F 62 8
Hastings to Ashford A 37 6
Hawick to Galashiels F 36 9
Hawkhurst - Branch Line to A 66 6
Hayling - Branch Line to A 12 3
Hay-on-Wye - BL around D 92 0
Haywards Heath to Seaford A 28 4
Hemel Hempstead - BLs to D 88 3
Henley, Windsor & Marlow - BLa C77 2
Hereford to Newport D 54 8
Hertford & Hatfield - BLs a E 58 1
Hertford Loop E 71 0
Hexham to Carlisle D 75 3
Hexham to Hawick F 08 6
Hitchin to Peterborough D 07 4
Horsham - Branch Lines to A 02 4
Hull, Hornsea and Withernsea G 27 2
Hull to Scarborough G 60 9
Huntingdon - Branch Line to A 93 2

I
Ilford to Shenfield C 97 0
Ilfracombe - Branch Line to B 21 3
Ilkeston to Chesterfield G 26 5
Inverkeithing to Thornton Jct G 76 0
Ipswich to Diss F 81 9
Ipswich to Saxmundham C 41 3
Isle of Man Railway Journey F 94 9
Isle of Wight Lines - 50 yrs C 12 3
Italy Narrow Gauge F 17 8

K
Kent Narrow Gauge C 45 1
Kettering to Nottingham F 82-6
Kidderminster to Shrewsbury E 10 9
Kingsbridge - Branch Line to C 98 7
Kings Cross to Potters Bar E 62 8
King's Lynn to Hunstanton F 58 1
Kingston & Hounslow Loops A 83 3
Kingswear - Branch Line to C 17 8

L
Lambourn - Branch Line to C 70 3
Lancaster to Oxenholme G 77 7
Launceston & Princetown - BLs C 19 2
Leeds to Selby G 47 0
Leek - Branch Line From G 01 2
Leicester to Burton F 85 7
Leicester to Nottingham G 15 9
Lewisham to Dartford A 92 5
Lincoln to Cleethorpes F 56 7
Lincoln to Doncaster G 03 6
Lines around Newmarket G 54 8
Lines around Stamford F 98 7
Lines around Wimbledon B 75 6
Lines North of Stoke G 29 6
Liverpool to Runcorn G 72 2
Liverpool Street to Chingford D 01 2
Liverpool Street to Ilford C 34 5
Llandeilo to Swansea E 46 8
London Bridge to Addiscombe B 20 6
London Bridge to East Croydon A 58 1
Longmoor - Branch Lines to A 41 3
Looe - Branch Line to C 22 2
Loughborough to Ilkeston G 24 1
Loughborough to Nottingham F 68 0
Lowestoft - BLs around E 40 6
Ludlow to Hereford E 14 7
Lydney - Branch Lines around E 26 0
Lyme Regis - Branch Line to A 45 1
Lynton - Branch Line to B 04 6

M
Machynlleth to Barmouth E 54 3
Maesteg and Tondu Lines F 06 2
Majorca & Corsica Narrow Gauge F 41 3
Manchester to Bacup G 46 3
Mansfield to Doncaster G 23 4
March - Branch Lines around B 09 1
Market Drayton - BLs around F 67 3
Market Harborough to Newark F 86 4
Marylebone to Rickmansworth D 49 4
Melton Constable to Yarmouth Bch E031
Midhurst - Branch Lines of E 78 9
Midhurst - Branch Lines to F 00 0
Minehead - Branch Line to A 80 2
Monmouth - Branch Lines to E 20 8
Monmouthshire Eastern Valleys D 71 5
Moretonhampstead - BL to C 27 7
Moreton-in-Marsh to Worcester D 26 5
Morpeth to Bellingham F 87 1
Mountain Ash to Neath D 80 7

N
Newark to Doncaster F 78 9
Newbury to Westbury C 66 6
Newcastle to Alnmouth G 36 4
Newcastle to Hexham D 69 2
Newmarket to Haughley & Laxfield G 71 5
New Mills to Sheffield G 44 9
Newport (IOW) - Branch Lines to A 26 0
Newquay - Branch Lines to C 71 0
Newton Abbot to Plymouth C 60 4
Newtown to Aberystwyth E 41 3
Northampton to Peterborough F 92 5
North East German NG D 44 9
Northern Alpine Narrow Gauge F 37 6
Northern Spain Narrow Gauge E 83 3
North London Line B 94 7
North of Birmingham F 55 0
North of Grimsby - Branch Lines G 09 8
North Woolwich - BLs around C 65 9
Nottingham to Boston F 70 3
Nottingham to Kirkby Bentinck G 38 8
Nottingham to Lincoln F 43 7
Nottingham to Mansfield G 52 4
Nuneaton to Loughborough G 08 1

O
Ongar - Branch Line to E 05 5
Orpington to Tonbridge B 03 9
Oswestry - Branch Lines around E 60 4
Oswestry to Whitchurch E 81 9
Oxford to Bletchley D 57 9
Oxford to Moreton-in-Marsh D 15 9

P
Paddington to Ealing C 37 6
Paddington to Princes Risborough C819
Padstow - Branch Line to B 54 1
Peebles Loop G 19 7
Pembroke and Cardigan - BLs to F 29 1
Peterborough to Kings Lynn E 32 1
Peterborough to Lincoln F 89 5
Peterborough to Newark F 72 7
Plymouth - BLs around B 98 5
Plymouth to St. Austell C 63 5
Pontypool to Mountain Ash D 65 4
Pontypridd to Merthyr F 14 7
Pontypridd to Port Talbot E 86 4
Porthmadog 1954-94 - BLa B 31 2
Portmadoc 1923-46 - BLa B 13 8
Portsmouth to Southampton A 31 4
Portugal Narrow Gauge E 67 3
Potters Bar to Cambridge D 70 8
Preston to Blackpool G 16 6
Preston to the Fylde Coast G 81 4
Preston to Lancaster G 74 6
Princes Risborough - BL to D 05 0
Princes Risborough to Banbury C 85 7

R
Railways to Victory C 16 1
Reading to Basingstoke B 27 5
Reading to Didcot C 79 6
Reading to Guildford A 47 5
Redhill to Ashford A 73 4
Return to Blaenau 1970-82 C 64 2
Rhyl to Bangor F 15 4
Rhymney & New Tredegar Lines E 48 2
Rickmansworth to Aylesbury D 61 6
Romania & Bulgaria NG E 23 9
Ross-on-Wye - BLs around E 30 7
Ruabon to Barmouth E 84 0
Rugby to Birmingham E 37 6
Rugby to Loughborough F 12 3
Rugby to Stafford F 07 9
Rugeley to Stoke-on-Trent F 90 1
Ryde to Ventnor A 19 2

S
Salisbury to Westbury B 39 8
Salisbury to Yeovil B 06 0
Sardinia and Sicily Narrow Gauge F 50 5
Saxmundham to Yarmouth C 69 7
Saxony & Baltic Germany Revisited F 71 0
Saxony Narrow Gauge D 47 0
Scunthorpe to Doncaster G 34 0
Seaton & Sidmouth - BLs to A 95 6
Selsey - Branch Line to A 04 8
Sheerness - Branch Line to B 16 2
Sheffield towards Manchester G 18 0
Shenfield to Ipswich E 96 3
Shildon to Stockton G 79 1
Shrewsbury - Branch Line to A 86 4
Shrewsbury to Chester E 70 3
Shrewsbury to Crewe F 48 2
Shrewsbury to Ludlow E 21 5
Shrewsbury to Newtown E 29 1
Sirhowy Valley Line E 12 3
Sittingbourne to Ramsgate A 90 1
Skegness & Mablethorpe - BL to F 84 0
Slough to Newbury C 56 7
South African Two-foot gauge E 51 2
Southampton to Bournemouth A 42 0
Southend & Southminster BLs E 76 5
Southern Alpine Narrow Gauge F 22 2
South London Line B 46 6
South Lynn to Norwich City F 03 1
Southwold - Branch Line to A 15 4
Spalding - Branch Lines around E 52 9
Spalding to Grimsby F 65 9 6
Stafford to Chester F 34 5
Stafford to Wellington F 59 8
St Albans to Bedford D 08 1
St. Austell to Penzance C 67 3
St. Boswell to Berwick F 44 4
Stourbridge to Wolverhampton E 16 1
St. Pancras to Barking D 68 5
St. Pancras to Folkestone E 88 8
St. Pancras to St. Albans C 78 9
Stratford to Cheshunt F 53 6
Stratford-u-Avon to Birmingham D 77 7
Stratford-u-Avon to Cheltenham C 25 3
Sudbury - Branch Lines to F 19 2
Surrey Narrow Gauge C 87 1
Sussex Narrow Gauge C 68 0
Swaffham - Branch Lines around F 97
Swanage to 1999 - BL to A 33 8
Swanley to Ashford B 45 9
Swansea - Branch Lines around F 38 3
Swansea to Carmarthen E 59 8
Swindon to Bristol C 96 3
Swindon to Gloucester D 46 3
Swindon to Newport D 30 2
Swiss Narrow Gauge C 94 9

T
Talyllyn 60 E 98 7
Tamworth to Derby F 76 5
Taunton to Barnstaple B 60 2
Taunton to Exeter C 82 6
Taunton to Minehead F 39 0
Tavistock to Plymouth B 88 6
Tenterden - Branch Line to A 21 5
Three Bridges to Brighton A 35 2
Tilbury Loop C 86 4
Tiverton - BLs around C 62 8
Tivetshall to Beccles D 41 8
Tonbridge to Hastings A 44 4
Torrington - Branch Lines to B 37 4
Tourist Railways of France G 04 3
Towcester - BLs around E 39 0
Tunbridge Wells BLs A 32 1

U
Upwell - Branch Line to B 64 0
Uttoxeter to Macclesfield G 05 0
Uttoxetor to Buxton G 33 3

V
Victoria to Bromley South A 98 7
Victoria to East Croydon A 40 6
Vivarais Revisited E 08 6

W
Walsall Routes F 45 1
Wantage - Branch Line to D 25 8
Wareham to Swanage 50 yrs D 09 8
Watercress Line G 75 3
Waterloo to Windsor A 54 3
Waterloo to Woking A 38 3
Watford to Leighton Buzzard D 45 6
Wellingborough to Leicester F 73 4
Welshpool to Llanfair E 49 9
Wenford Bridge to Fowey C 09 3
Wennington to Morecambe G 58 6
Westbury to Bath B 55 8
Westbury to Taunton C 76 5
West Cornwall Mineral Rlys D 48 7
West Croydon to Epsom B 08 4
West German Narrow Gauge D 93 7
West London - BLs of C 50 5
West London Line B 84 8
West Somerset Railway G 78 4
West Wiltshire - BLs of D 12 8
Weymouth - BLs A 65 9
Willesden Jn to Richmond B 71 8
Wimbledon to Beckenham C 58 1
Wimbledon to Epsom B 62 6
Wimborne - BLs around A 97 0
Wirksworth - Branch Lines to G 10 4
Wisbech - BLs around C 01 7
Witham & Kelvedon - BLs a E 82 6
Woking to Alton A 59 8
Woking to Portsmouth A 25 3
Woking to Southampton A 55 0
Wolverhampton to Shrewsbury E 44
Wolverhampton to Stafford F 79 6
Worcester to Birmingham D 97 5
Worcester to Hereford D 38 8
Worthing to Chichester A 06 2
Wrexham to New Brighton F 47 5
Wroxham - BLs around F 31 4

Y
Yeovil - 50 yrs change C 38 3
Yeovil to Dorchester A 76 5
Yeovil to Exeter A 91 8
York to Scarborough F 23 9